Living in His Presence

Living in His Presence. Copyright ©2006, 2008, 2009 by Gina Moroney.

Protected by the copyright laws of the United States of America. All rights reserved. No other part of this book may be reproduced in any form or by any electronic or mechanical means including information storage and retrieval systems without permission in writing from the publisher, except by a review, who may quote brief passages in a review.

Library of Congress Cataloging-in-Publication Data: Moroney, Gina.
LCN: 2008937232
ISBN: 978-1-934749-33-3

Published by: *Cross House Publishing, www.crosshousepublishing.org*

Book cover and page production: *Blue Dot Creative, www.bluedotcreative.com*

Scripture quotations from Nelson's New King James version Study Bible (NKJV), copyright ©1997 by Thomas Nelson, Inc. Used by permission.

Prayer Poems by Gina Moroney.

This edition printed on acid-free paper.

Printed in the United States of America.

Living in His Presence

EXPERIENCE THE REALITY OF GOD

Gina Moroney

Foreword by Ruth Myers

Cross House Publishing

For Ruth,

Beloved author of many timeless Christian books and Bible studies…
The Lord used you to inspire <u>Living in His Presence</u>.
May He reward you with measures of blessing,
more plentiful than you can count!

I give glory to God the Father who inspired and trusted me to write *Living in His Presence*. God met me on every avenue that I explored in the writing process. He opened doors, led the way, and protected me. He is worthy of all my praise!

acknowledgements

Words are powerful, and they penetrate the heart. Yet there are moments when it seems like words aren't enough to portray our deepest sentiments. Surely you know the feeling! One of those moments is creeping up on me right now as I try to express what is in my heart to those who have impacted my life and *Living in His Presence*. Even as I stumble a bit with my own words, I pray that God would empower these simple thanks and place my sincere gratitude within the hearts of those I love.

Mike…thank you for your unfailing love, leadership, and spiritual maturity in our marriage. You are my hero who inspirits me to go deeper with Christ.

Ryan, Amber and Jim…your acceptance and unconditional love for me exemplify the character of Jesus. Thank you for loving your mom so. You are the greatest!

Chris and Marilyn…thank you for leading the way to the Lord and for the priceless times we spend together.

Chuck and Deb…you introduced our family to Jesus. You pour spiritual truth into our lives, and you model Christianity for us. Thank you.

Karen…out of the kindness of your heart, you read, re-read, and offered cherished advice for this book. Thank you for giving of yourself to help make this possible.

Abbey…you have been a sweet, valuable resource. Thank you.

Gail…you listened to the voice of God, and He used your obedient heart to help make *Living in His Presence* possible. Thank you.

My wonderful friends…you know who you are, and you know how dear you are to me. You believed this project was of God from the start and encouraged me with your enthusiasm, love, and prayers. Thank you.

"I thank my God upon every remembrance of you."
(Philippians 1:3)

foreword

In a world where busyness and stress run rampant in the lives of many, it is reassuring to know that our precious Lord is tangible and ever present for those who seek Him. We serve a personal God who is ready and willing to reveal Himself to us in marvelous new ways as we follow Him.

The Scriptures portray a beautiful relationship between the Triune God and His people. God the Father, in His infinite mind, conceived the idea of relating and shared it with the world when He created man. Jesus Christ, His Son, fulfilled this idea of His God/man relationship when He lived here on earth. Now the Holy Spirit opens the way for a personal relationship with the Triune God, making it possible for us to experience God's presence and live with Him day by day.

Living in His Presence can help bring the reality of God's presence into our everyday lives. This book is a practical approach for learning to live with God, moment by moment. It will appeal to you because it takes a look at real life. It is refreshing and enjoyable. It gives an account of Gina's spiritual journey as she learned to listen for the voice of God, to know Him more intimately. As you read her stories and glean from their insights, you will grow spiritually and be enriched.

While you read, be sure to be alert for the Lord to manifest His presence in new ways so that you can embrace more of His reality. Let Gina's transparency about her Christian faith paint a vivid picture of the childlike faith the Bible tells us we must have. Allow yourself to relate to her and to the life lessons that have helped her develop spiritually.

In this book you will find many prayers that can enhance your journey with God. Use these prayers again and again. Let them lead you into a richer walk with our wonderful three-person God—Father, Son, and Holy Spirit. As you feed on each page, take time to pray about and absorb the life-changing truths that it presents. Pray as Hudson Taylor did,

"Lord Jesus, make Yourself to me

A living bright reality

More present to faith's vision keen

Than any earthy object seen,

More dear, more intimately nigh,

Than e'en the sweetest earthly tie."

Our gracious Lord will bless you and enrich your spiritual life as you experience *Living in His Presence*. It is a "must read" if you are looking for fresh and real encounters with God.

~ *Ruth Myers*

before you begin... an invitation

Who do you say that Jesus Christ is? Was He merely a great man who lived over 2000 years ago, or is He the Son of God, the Messiah, your Savior? Is Jesus the way to everlasting life? How you will experience *Living in His Presence* depends upon what you believe to be true about Jesus Christ. Jesus **is** the Son of the one true God, and Jesus is alive. His Spirit dwells in the hearts of all those who believe in Him and have invited Him to be their personal Lord and Savior. Jesus paid the price and died for your sins and mine. He rose from the dead so that we may have a right relationship with God the Father and live forever with Him in Heaven someday. Jesus is God's free gift of salvation to the world. There's nothing you can do to earn salvation; it is a gift of love.

Perhaps you have never invited Jesus to be your personal Savior, or you have felt undeserving of God's gift of salvation. Maybe you believe that Jesus is the Son of God but have never entered into a relationship with Him. You might feel like you once had a relationship with Jesus, but somehow you've distanced yourself from Him. If you are nodding your head, then I encourage you to take a step of faith; take a closer look at Jesus Christ in the Bible. The most famous scripture of the Bible reads: *"For God so loved the world that He gave His only begotten Son that whoever believes in Him should not perish but have everlasting life"* (John 3:16). When Jesus began His ministry, He said, *"The time is fulfilled, and the kingdom of God is at hand. Repent, and believe in the gospel"* (Mark 1:15). Jesus responded to a man who wanted to understand more about Him. Jesus said, *"Most assuredly, I say to you, unless one is born again, he cannot see the kingdom of God"* (John 3:3). Believe, repent, and experience spiritual rebirth; then you will be saved! This is the reality of the good news of the gospel for you and for me.

The following prayer is a first time prayer of salvation for spiritual rebirth. It is also a rededication prayer for those who have already been spiritually reborn. The prayer reminds me of who Jesus is, who I am, where I've come from, and where I am going. It is a prayer of deep conviction, of salvation. Whether it is your first time to pray this type of prayer or not, these are powerful words that need to come from your heart. The power behind this prayer opens up the flood gates of Heaven to welcome you into God's kingdom where His children will live forever one day with Jesus Christ. You will be empowered to walk with Jesus on this earth and live for Him. If you sense that Christ is drawing you near, then please turn the page, and join me in prayer.

PRAYER OF SALVATION

Dear Heavenly Father, I know that I am a sinner and that I've sinned many times. Jesus, You are the Son of God, and You came to earth to save me from the consequences of my sins. You died on the cross for my sins, and then You rose from the dead so that I may enter into a right relationship with God and live in Heaven with You forever. Please forgive me of my sins, and thank you that You do. Thank you for Your grace, that undeserved mercy You extend to me, which covers all of my sins. Please come into my life now, be the Lord of my life, and please help me to be the person You want me to be. I invite You, Jesus, to live within my heart, and I ask You to send Your Holy Spirit to be with me. Thank you that Your Holy Spirit will never leave me nor forsake me. I belong to You, Jesus, and You are my Lord and Savior forever. Thank you! Amen.

Years ago, I prayed a prayer much like this one and was spiritually reborn into the Kingdom of God. That day, I began a wonderful journey which changed my life. Living in His Presence recalls that journey, and I share it with you now.

New Beginning

THE SECRET...Uncovered Treasure

A LIFE CHANGING EVENT MIGHT BE RARE AND FLEETING, but the memory always lingers as a milestone marked on the timeline of life. I can still see a specific milestone highlighted in bold print on my timeline of events, the moment I was reborn spiritually and accepted Jesus Christ as my personal Lord and Savior. My life changed on that monumental day when I felt the presence of God as never before. God touched me in a powerful way; His presence was unmistakably real, and I knew life would never be the same.

How **would** my life change? Where would that amazing, first encounter with God take me? I felt an instant hunger to grow spiritually, but I had many questions about the Christian life and didn't know how to begin. A caring young pastor and his wife, Chuck and Deb, witnessed my conversion to Christianity and were instrumental in my spiritual growth. They encouraged me to attend a church with solid Biblical teaching, to read my Bible faithfully everyday, and spend time with other Christians.

Chuck and Deb became my mentors and drove two hours every week for more than a year, pouring every spiritual insight and experience they had, into my life. They helped me to understand that Christianity is more than simply believing in Jesus Christ. It is a lifestyle of pursuing God through a vibrant relationship with Jesus by way of the Holy Spirit. That was headline news to me! A relationship with Christ had to mean that I could operate on a personal level with God. Learning about God and praying to Him wasn't going to be enough anymore; there was more to Christianity that I had been missing. For the first time, I began to realize that God has always longed for a loving relationship with me.

Chuck and Deb continued to model Christianity, and I watched them with intensity. They had something I desired, and I wouldn't settle for anything less than everything they had acquired in their Christian lives. Oftentimes I listened to them talk about what God had spoken at certain times, and I was intrigued. What did they mean when they said, "God told us?" I needed to understand more. That is when my faithful mentors shared a precious secret with me about God. It was like discovering a hidden treasure. I will always remember my excitement when they cracked open the lid on the spiritual treasure chest and uncovered portions of the secret for me. I learned that when they prayed, they also listened for God's voice through His Holy Spirit. At first I thought perhaps they had the privilege of hearing God's voice because they are pastors who shepherd those attending their church. But they told me that prayer is a two way communication system, an intimate act of communion with God for **anyone** who is reborn spiritually. That meant **me**! I recall a specific prayer when I asked God to show me if this was real enough for me, and He answered my prayer. A supernatural light went on, and I felt the presence of God shining deep within my heart, nudging me to engage in conversation with Him. My joy was hard to contain, for I knew I was about to embark on an exciting journey pursuing God through prayer and fellowship. This would become my passion in life.

My mentors stayed right there with me. They reinforced my need to read the Bible faithfully as a staple of life and helped me to practice "tuning in," asking simple questions of God, expecting an answer. This proved to be an excellent training ground as I learned to recognize the voice of God's Holy Spirit in the daily circumstances of life. My workouts on the training field proved to be worthwhile when I even began to hear God's voice at critical times. Hearing from the King of Kings, the most significant One of all times was not to be taken for granted. I lived to hear from God, and His will soon became my desire. My mentors encouraged me to work at "fine tuning" my new prayer life. At times I wondered if I was hearing from God. I thought perhaps it was just my mind and emotions, but I continued with my intense pursuit of God. Eventually I could hear Him whisper the kindest, most lovely words to me. Yes, The Lord would even initiate conversation with me. God was about to become my best friend; what a privilege!

God desires an intimate friendship with every Christian, a lifetime of knowing Him. The Bible says that Jesus is the Shepherd, and we are His flock. In John 10:3, 4 Jesus says,

"...the sheep hear his voice; and he calls his own sheep by name and leads them out. And when he brings out his own sheep, he goes before them; and the sheep follow him, for they know his voice." It sounds as if Jesus is expecting us to listen for Him when He says that His sheep **know** His voice. How exciting to anticipate the voice of the Good Shepherd! Lives are transformed when relationships with the Lord mature to immeasurable depths of intimacy, and His children grow to know Him better.

Listening for the voice of the Holy Spirit is only the beginning. There is more to the secret...God not only wants to have fellowship with us, but He desires this fellowship to be moment by moment. We don't have to hope we can hear from God occasionally; His Spirit is alive in each of us, and our conversations with God will be ongoing. Pursue God through continuous fellowship with Him, and He will dramatically improve the quality of your Christian life. Be encouraged to take a stroll down the path of knowing Him better. You will find yourself running, as in a sprint, to meet God more on the streets and avenues of your daily life.

Imagine having a close friendship with the most high profile, powerful person in the world. Wouldn't you jump at every invitation to be with that person? I know that I would clear my calendar for such an opportunity. The most noble, influential One of all times lovingly extends a standing invitation to be with Him and then spiritually draws us unto Himself. That is exciting! Jeremiah, the prophet, said: *"The Lord has appeared of old to me, saying 'Yes, I have loved you with an everlasting love; therefore with loving kindness I have drawn you'"* (Jeremiah 31:3). What joy to feel the Lord's love as He draws you into His presence!

Clear the calendars of your mind and the busy schedules of your heart, and accept this gracious invitation to pursue the King. Hebrews 10:22 reads, *"Let us draw near with a true heart in full assurance of faith."* In drawing near we are assured that He is with us in difficult times and that His goodness never leaves us. *"Surely goodness and mercy shall follow me all the days of my life; and I will dwell in the house of the Lord forever"* (Psalm 23:6).

Is it possible to live in the presence of the Almighty? We work at getting into His presence occasionally. Perhaps during quiet devotional times or on spiritual retreats we feel the presence of God. We talk about when God "showed up" during a special song or hymn and how we invited His presence into the room. But staying in God's presence and flourishing there is foreign to many of us. Does anyone actually live this way? There are those today whom we don't hear much about, yet they quietly practice living in God's presence. Many have read the writings of Brother Lawrence and Madame Jean Guyon from the seventeenth century who practiced the presence of God. Their lives were testimonies of unquestionable awareness of Christ. Frank Laubach was a missionary to the Philippines, author, and beloved teacher in the twentieth century. He had a deep, consistent awareness of the Lord. Mother Teresa served the Lord, always in His presence. These devoted Christians pursued their Maker. They lived with Him and knew Him. In the midst of their dutiful lives they chose the Lord Jesus Christ to be their constant companion.

The twenty-first century presents everyone with more busyness than ever, but there is always time to enjoy companionship with

God. The Lord desires for you to live with Him and have great fellowship no matter how busy you become. He calls you to a life of fellowship with Him in 1Corinthians1:9. *"God is faithful, by whom you were called into the fellowship of His Son, Jesus Christ our Lord."* As the Lord calls, He is also faithful. He empowers you to live with Him regardless of your busyness. It becomes your choice. It is His desire and your choice. The joys of knowing God are immeasurable. The comfort of His companionship is indescribable in times of loneliness and difficulty. Perhaps this sounds inviting but not attainable. You might have the will to live in the presence of God but can't figure out the way to get there. The Lord, Himself, is the Way. He draws you unto Himself just the way you are when you desire Him. Imperfect as we are, God makes it possible for everyone to arrive at the final destination, day by day. I know that my relationship with my Best Friend will always be a work in progress as I continue to grow and seek Him.

Learning to live in the continual presence of God is a journey. It takes time to cultivate an intimate relationship with the Lord. I have found that the journey is really the goal. Sometimes it is as if I am set on cruise control, and I am riding along. Other times it feels like I am stuck in a traffic jam. But the memories along the way and the lessons I learn are priceless.

I must admit that while I was inspired by the writings of those who lived in the presence of God, I still needed to understand **how** they got there. I asked God to show me practical ways to live with Him moment by moment. The Holy Spirit revealed five specific ingredients that I must incorporate into my life to help experience His presence more and more. Beginning with the first ingredient, the rest build upon each other making it possible to add them in one by one for the journey. The next five chapters of this book discuss each one of those five ingredients. In the last chapter, we will take a peek at what living in the presence of God could be like. There are times to pause throughout this book in order to provide opportunity for prayer and reflection. Take time to meditate upon the scriptures and "prayer poems." They are meant to be like fragrant aromas, helping you draw near to God. Perhaps you have other meaningful ingredients to embellish your journey. Certainly godly virtues, principles, and other scriptures will add to your awareness of the Lord's presence.

This book is personal, written as if you and I are having a meaningful conversation. You will come to know me as I share my spiritual life with you. I hope that you can draw from the insights and lessons that I learned from God as well as from my doubts and the mistakes that I've made along the way. There are many well known spiritual giants whom I have learned from. I admire them and could quote their famous writings. Yet because this is a story of my journey, I chose to reference a few of those who have walked on the path with me. They have had a profound impact on my life, and you will meet them.

Living in His presence is about spiritual growth, experiencing the reality of God. There's no hurry to finish reading it. Allow the Holy Spirit to guide you through the pages, and do take time to absorb and digest all that God has for you. Cultivate your relationship with God, and savor every moment as you go. Perhaps later on, you will want to reference parts of the book for encouragement as you practice living in the presence of God.

I know that the Holy Spirit prompts me to go back and look at the "prayer poems" or read over portions of each chapter when I need to be strengthened along the way. You are not on this journey alone; the Holy Spirit is your perfect guide, living and working in you. He will direct your path.

Draw near to God through Jesus Christ, and journey with me to nurture a meaningful life with Him. The narrow path of getting to know God better opens up to an interstate of living in His presence. Wide, open lanes are cleared for all who desire to travel there. The spiritual blessings are abundant, and lofty milestones appear on every timeline. I pray that God will lay spiritual milestones on the timeline of your life as you journey and learn to live in His presence.

"...being confident of this very thing, that He who has begun a good work in you will complete it until the day of Jesus Christ." (Philippians1: 6)

One

PRAISE AND THANKSGIVING...Attitude of Gratitude

You cause my heart to overflow with joy.
My mind is filled with heavenly purpose.
My flesh shall cease of its insistence.
Behold, these tears of joy as the old fades away
And the new is ushered in with righteousness!
I am a new self, a new proclamation,
A new attitude and way of life.
I cast off the old and worn and dress in what is new,
The true garment of praise, joy, peace, and laughter.
The fragrance of sweet roses is upon me,
Freshly picked, dripping with the dew of Your anointing,
Ready to be planted in the spot that Your have set for me.
Such joy, I have never known before,
Such joy shall always be familiar to me!

THE JOURNEY BEGINS WITH PRAISE AND THANKSGIVING. This is when the mind and heart unite spiritually with God to experience Him. In a spirit of intimacy God draws each one close in oneness with Him. Yet as we approach God in oneness, we must remember that **He is still God.** He is the Creator of all things and reigns sovereign over all thrones! My sister, Marilyn, loves to sing beautiful praises to God. She once reminded me of how sometimes we get too comfortable with God and forget just who He is. She said that we reach a place where we are up close and personal but tend to overlook His sovereignty and forget about the reverence He deserves. Never lose sight of God's sovereignty or His power and authority to rule. God the Father is the One in charge, and we must love and respect Him at all times. He is supreme, yet perfectly loving at the same time and worthy of our praise. *"You are worthy, O Lord, to receive glory and honor and power; for You created all things, and by Your will they exist and were created"* (Revelation 4: 11).

There have been many kings and kingdoms over time, but our relationship is with the King of all the other kings and His kingdom will never end. Our King rules with power and authority but not with an iron fist. There are no unrealistic expectations or threats upon our lives. God simply asks that we love Him and give Him all of our praise. Jesus said, *"Love the Lord your God with all your heart and with all your soul and with all your mind. This is the first and greatest commandment"* (Matthew 22: 37). How marvelous that we have the joy and privilege of loving God and indulging in **His** love! We can't help but walk closer in intimacy with God. Our praiseful walk paves the path on the journey to live in God's presence while the Holy Spirit guides the way.

The greatness of our God ushers in thoughts of excellence that transpire your mind. He **is** worthy of all praise!

THOUGHTS OF EXCELLENCE
Casting my eyes upon You
I see the world as You do.
First, I contemplate Your love
Then I fix my eyes upon Your truth and nobility,
Your righteousness, purity, loveliness, and what is admirable.
I think of such excellence, worthy of praise!
When I think and contemplate this way, You transpire my mind
That Your goodness may infuse my memory cells.
My memory and what I feel
Is filtered by Your love and goodness.
Only in Your strength I may think this way,
Always in Your strength I shall feel this way.
My life is about Your love...
To reflect Your love always.

"Great is the Lord, and greatly to be praised
In the city of our God,
In His holy mountain." (Psalm 48:1)

My journey on the path began when I felt the Lord urging me to get up every morning to begin my day with praise songs unto Him. Was that really the Holy Spirit speaking, I wondered? It seemed to **me** that a good devotional or Bible study was a more appropriate, spiritual way to begin each day. Nevertheless, I knew that God was drawing me, and I sensed that great intimacy would result from my obedient act of praise. I thought of times in the Bible when God's people praised Him and mighty things happened. During those times, His power and presence were unmistakable.

One of my favorite stories about praising God that is in the Bible is found in the book of Acts in chapter 16. Paul was with Silas who was a prophet and leader among the Christians. They were stripped, beaten, and imprisoned in chains for teaching about their faith in Jesus Christ. Here is what the Bible says: *"But at midnight Paul and Silas were praying and singing hymns to God and the prisoners were listening to them. Suddenly there was a great earthquake, so that the foundations of the prison were shaken; and immediately all the doors were opened and everyone's chains were loosed. And the keeper of the prison, awaking from sleep and seeing the prison doors opened, supposing the prisoners had fled, drew his sword and was about to kill himself. But Paul called with a loud voice, saying, 'Do yourself no harm, for we are all here.' Then he called for a light, ran in, and fell down trembling before Paul and Silas. And he brought them out and said, 'Sirs, what must I do to be saved?' So they said, 'Believe on the Lord Jesus Christ, and you will be saved, you and your household'"* (Acts 16: 25-31). Oh to be a little mouse in the corner and witness their praise and then the awesome display of God's enormous power!

The more I encountered powerful stories from the Bible, my anticipation and hunger grew for God's presence. Would I see incredible miracles? Would my house rumble and shake at the unmistakable presence of The Almighty? I desired to experience God just as Biblical characters did long ago. Soon I was praising God each morning in a quiet place with my favorite Christian music, open to worship Him however He desired. There were times when I danced before God and times when I couldn't help but lie flat on my face in reverence to Him. I could make a fool of myself, and no one knew except God; He seemed to enjoy my spontaneity. It felt right to be there before God as He filled my heart with joy.

Times alone with God continued to be joyful as I met Him daily. With no distractions and no one watching, there is an incredible freedom to reach out and touch the God of the Universe. I chose to reach out to Him no matter how uncomfortable it felt, and I praised God any way I could. My simple times of worship must have touched God, for **He** began to come and touch **my** heart. I worshiped, and He came to me! It is a blessing I never anticipated, yet treasure more than words can express. It wasn't even necessary to end my times of praise with a special kind of prayer or reading from the Bible, for our times together became like prayer when I joined with God, heart to heart.

Sometimes I questioned what I was doing and what was happening. I thought maybe I should wake up and learn more about God or do more for Him. But the Holy Spirit continued to draw me into this time of intimacy with Him instead. I learned to make time later in the day for more traditional prayer and

Bible study. My learning curve about God took off like a rocket on a mission. I craved God and fixed my eyes on a destination place. One day I would arrive in that place of abundance in His presence, and praising Him taught me more than I expected. I learned that God is real and tangible; His love for us is genuine. I realized that His anointing upon us and His desire for us are stronger than any passion or need we conjure up. The freedom to experience intimacy with God opened spiritual doors to invite His anointing into my life as never before. It was like having a taste of heaven. Just one taste, and my appetite increased for God.

Open the door and invite the Lord's anointing to transform your life. You are never empty…you overflow in Him!

ANOINTING

I meditate on these words, murmuring them again and again.
I know Your anointing is upon my head, my very life!
I will overflow with all that has been poured into me.
Words of praise and thanksgiving I utter to You
For they are on my tongue always.
May I freely give out all that has been given to me,
Be a blessing and a messenger of hope and love,
A true ambassador on Your behalf.
I shall overflow with all that has been poured into me,
Never to be empty as long as I walk in Your anointing.
It is endless, for truly goodness and love will follow me
All the days of my life!

"You anoint my head with oil, my cup overflows."
(Psalm 23:5)

Before long I eagerly anticipated the presence and faithfulness of God in every nook and cranny of my life. God was drawing me, and my relationship moved from the shallow end to the deeper waters of obedience. As wonderful as that might sound, there were times when I preferred to sleep longer and missed out on precious times with the Lord. Other times, I battled my heavy eyes and fought my will so I could get up to be with God. The Bible instructs us to make a sacrifice of praise. *"Therefore by Him let us continually offer a sacrifice of praise to God, that is the fruit of our lips, giving thanks to His name"* (Hebrews 13:15). In that obedient sacrifice of praise, the Holy Spirit softened my heart to love and desire Him more. The Bible also says that God inhabits our praise. His luxurious love and joy saturates our hearts, and praise overflows to bear good fruit for God with rewards that last a lifetime. Remember the story about Paul and Silas in prison? In the midst of their suffering they must have offered up a true sacrifice of praise. God inhabited their praise, and something wonderful came from that. The prison guard and his family became believers and followers of Jesus Christ. Just imagine the joy that Paul and Silas must have experienced. It all started with a heart of praise unto the Lord.

More than a year passed when the Holy Spirit prompted me to praise God each morning in ways other than song. I read aloud from the Bible, meditated on the Psalms, and kept a journal of my heartfelt thoughts of praise for the Father and His Son, Jesus. All God really cared about was obedience and commitment to be with Him, and He inhabited whatever form of praise I engaged in. For some, morning is best to spend quality time praising God, and for others it might not work out quite as well. The Lord knows when your best time of day is and will draw you as He desires. Your best time might vary depending on schedules and your lifestyle. God might even choose to change your schedules or lifestyle so that He may direct your path and take it from there. Most importantly, make yourself available in an attitude of praise and thanksgiving. The attitude of praise that you have in your special moments with God will infiltrate the hours that follow. That praiseful posture becomes a way of life.

Praising God and living in an attitude of gratefulness becomes your lifestyle, a fresh, new way to live. Everything we do can glorify God and keep Him with us each moment. How you enjoy God and give to Him is up to you and the Holy Spirit. Yes, the Spirit of God even directs your praise if you allow Him to do so. It is an outflow of your love for Him. God will bring you to a place where your whole body and everything you do praises Him. *"Bless the Lord, O my soul; And all that is within me, bless His holy name"* (Psalm 103:1).

When we live in an attitude of praise and thanksgiving, we remember the good gifts and precious things that God has given to each of us. *"Every good gift and every perfect gift is from above, and comes down from the Father of Lights"* (James 1:17). Acts of kindness come our way often, and gratitude always follows. A gift is almost always welcome, and it comes with a double helping of blessing because the generosity of the giver comes along with the gift. It's a pleasure to think about those who have done amazing things for us out of the kindness of their hearts, especially if we have done nothing to warrant such goodness.

So it is with the Lord. *"The works of the Lord are great, studied by all who have pleasure in them. He has made His wonderful works to be remembered"* (Psalm 111: 2, 4). God is the inventor of good works. Surely we will praise Him when we look around and see His splendor in all of creation. Remembering His marvelous deeds, you will melt in His arms and embrace His majesty.

God's marvelous deeds spring from the depths of His love. Your life is an expression of your love and gratitude for Christ. His love becomes your love.

EXPRESSIONS OF LOVE

Marvelous, a word for Your wonderful works,
But no word may truly express the wonder of Your works,
The majesty of Your character, the splendor of Your divinity
Or the depth of Your love.
Such wonder, majesty, splendor and love
I can't express just with words…
But in heartfelt gratitude and open expressions of love to You.
My life will express Your love
In a spirit of gratitude all about me.
For Your very character, O Lord,
Is expressed in actions, not only in words,
Revealing true love, humility, and abundant gratitude.

"Praise be to the Lord God, the God of Israel,
Who alone does marvelous deeds." (Psalm 72: 18)

Allow yourself to ponder the Lord throughout the day. The choice to think about Him is a key that opens the door of praise and thanksgiving where gratitude and love are there to greet you. When God is on my mind, I can see and praise Him everywhere. In every circumstance throughout the day, think of God and give thanks. At first, it doesn't come naturally. Sometimes living life this way takes us out of the comfort zone. Letting go and moving beyond what is normal is a stretch. But make a choice to see things through the eyes of God, and then the Holy Spirit will help you live a life of praise and thanksgiving. It's God's desire, and He knows that we will rejoice over and again as we grow closer to Him. *"Rejoice in the Lord always. Again I will say, rejoice"* (Philippians 4: 4). An attitude of gratitude helps me to love and praise the Lord in whatever I do.

Almost everywhere we go we are exposed to music, mostly songs with lyrics about love. Well, God **is** love and the author of love. When we are in love with Him, it is easy to turn any love song into a praiseful offering to the Lord, but it is still uplifting to listen to Christian music whenever possible. The Lord loves it when we make the best out of daily life and take every opportunity to bring Him glory. He doesn't care what we use, only that we draw near. He will inhabit whatever praise we offer to Him. A praiseful attitude of the heart enables us to enter into worship no matter what is going on around us. We go on with our normal, daily routines and take God with us. This **is** living in the presence of God.

Those who draw close to God in praise and thanksgiving quietly attract the attention of others. People want what we have even if they don't know what it is. They sense something different about someone who is madly in love with Jesus Christ. It's as if their eyes make a connection and want to follow you home to understand more about you. It is a part of the character of Jesus that is subconsciously irresistible. Who knows what God is doing? We do know that He uses everything for His glory! *"He has put a new song in my mouth...Praise to our God; many will see it and fear, and will trust in the Lord"* (Psalm 40: 3). Living with an attitude of gratefulness and praise brings out the joy of the Lord within us. It has a positive effect on others. People enjoy being around those who naturally radiate the joy of the Lord. It becomes contagious as others want what we have. Ultimately, God is glorified!

The one who lives in a praiseful attitude is also more likely to resist sin and temptation. If your mind is on God and its focus is on living with Him, it becomes more resistant to evil, and you draw closer to Him. The Bible tells us to draw near to God and that He will draw near to us. Think about it. God does not embrace evil, therefore when we cling to Him we flee from sin. That doesn't mean that we never sin. We all stumble and fall, but thankfully we always have forgiveness through our Lord Jesus Christ when we repent. Nothing will keep us from God. Your thankful heart steers clear of evil with God's help.

"And my tongue shall speak of Your righteousness And of Your praise all the day long" (Psalm 35: 28). What about at night? Is it possible to praise God while you are asleep? Absolutely! Get in the habit of going to bed with a praiseful scripture in mind. Read it aloud and then murmur that scripture while falling asleep.

If you wake up, practice thinking about God and whisper a word or two to Him, even momentarily. You'll feel His presence and know that He is with you while you sleep. When I awake and see that the alarm clock is not ready to ring, I am always relieved. What a perfect time to offer a word of love or gratitude to God before falling back to sleep! God is not asleep; His presence never leaves. God cherishes every word of love and gratitude as we acknowledge Him. Psalm 63: 6 reads so beautifully. *"When I remember You on my bed, I meditate on You in the night watches."* Oftentimes, when I invite the Lord to stay with me through the night, I awake in an attitude of gratitude making it easy to focus on Him right away. Talk to God when you first wake up in the morning because He is waiting for you, real and always present. Don't forget about Him; keep your eyes upon God during the day **and** night.

God's eyes are forever upon you. God never slumbers, nor does He sleep. He is there for you. Lift your eyes, and see Him alone.

EYES UPON YOU

I give You my worship,
All of my praise.
Lifting my eyes to your throne
I see You and You alone.
With my eyes upon You
There is nothing too big.
Nothing's impossible for me.
No mountain is too high,
No valley too low.
I shall soar and overcome weakness,
Yes, even overcome and surpass my own strength.
As I give You my worship, all of my praise,
I shall lift my eyes to your throne.
I see You and You alone.

"I will lift my eyes to the hills—From whence comes my help? My help comes from the Lord who made heaven and earth. He will not allow your foot to be moved; He who keeps you will not slumber." (Psalm 121:1-3)

It is much easier to include God when you make the effort to focus on Him. You will lay a firm foundation to help live in the awareness of God's presence. There is much to be grateful for when you choose to take an honest look at your life. My husband, Mike, is a realistic optimist and a true encouragement to me when he reminds me of how important it is to see the glass half full of water instead of half empty. It changes my attitude. Choose to see the good over the not so good, and the glass becomes full. This attitude allows you to see that life is full of abundance.

The Bible says that everything that is good comes from God. Even the good things that you accomplish are ultimately because of God and His great work in you. Don't take the credit or glory for anything you do. Instead, acknowledge the Lord and give Him the credit. It doesn't matter how great or small the success, it isn't you; **it is God**. Some would disagree and call this false humility, but true humility speaks out loud to say that apart from God, we can do nothing good. Humility is a key attitude before God, and prideful attitudes diminish so that Christ may increase. Humility does well in the presence of God. It opens another door for the Holy Spirit to become an integral part of our lives. Jesus is the true vine, and we are the branches. He says, *"I am the vine, you are the branches. He who abides in Me, and I in him, bears much fruit; for without Me you can do nothing"* (John 15: 5). We bring honor to God when we give Him the credit that is rightfully His. Jesus even said, *"I do nothing of Myself, but as My Father taught Me. If I honor Myself, My honor is nothing"* (John 8: 28, 54).

Honoring God becomes a comfort to you because you are no longer out there in the world on your own. I would much rather have God working within me than be working my way through life alone. My self-confidence escalates when it is in Christ. I don't mind giving God the credit; **He** deserves it, and there is always a better outcome. Eventually there will be no ownership or self-pride in anything you do. That doesn't mean you shouldn't strive for excellence or claim your work and take pride in it. It simply gives you a better reason to enjoy what you accomplish. It keeps you humble, and that is a healthy place to be when pursuing a relationship with God.

Give God the praise and thanksgiving He deserves. When He sits at the control panels of your life, His Spirit becomes a life long companion bringing light across your path. On that path you can spot the interstate of living in His presence. It isn't far away, and praising God continually will bring you closer. Choose to praise the Lord with your life, and you will advance down the path to live in the presence of God.

"My praise shall be continually of You. Let my mouth be filled with Your praise And with Your glory all the day. And I will praise you yet, more and more." (Psalm 71: 6, 8, 14)

Two

PRAYER AND COMMUNICATION...Loving Fellowship

*How true...where You go I may also come.
Where I go, there You are like an eternal friendship.
Oh, that we may become one for I desire it so.
You know me and remember me
Every minute of my life.
When I sleep or wake, sit or stand...
If I feel You there or not, You are with me.
How much more wonderful to be aware of You always,
More productive, content, joyful, and restful.
Yes, I will tune in to Your presence.
For You long to be with me more than anyone does.
I'm created to know You, seek You, my God,
And live in Your sweet presence.
It is meant to be so.*

FELLOWSHIP WITH GOD IS ONE OF THE GREATEST JOYS WE HAVE as followers of Jesus Christ. What a privilege to hear from the most influential One of all time as He calls us into fellowship through Jesus Christ. *"God is faithful, by whom you were called into the fellowship of His Son, Jesus Christ our Lord"* (1 Corinthians 1: 9). This is what we were created for. God longs to share His heart with us as we open ours to Him. When we live with an attitude of thanksgiving and praise, there is more of a focus on God; He becomes real, and the desire to communicate with Him grows strong. Many shy away from God with the perception that He is "out there," too busy with the urgencies of the world. How can the Creator of all things have time for each of us, some would ask? Yes, He is busy with the needs of the world, but **He is God**. God is omnipresent and loving.

In Matthew 10:30, Jesus said that the very hairs of our heads are all numbered. God is so personal that He actually lives in each of our hearts and calls each of us by a special name. The Lord cares deeply about every detail of your life and lovingly waits for you to call. Just one connection with God, and you will begin to understand the reality of His presence in your life and desire to communicate with Him one on one. In the Bible, we learn of how Jesus spent a great deal of time in prayer, listening for the voice of the Father. He lived in constant fellowship with the Father seeking the will of God. Jesus had great influence and changed the world. If each of us lived in His presence, in constant fellowship with the Father, we would be effective as well. Certainly we'll do our part to be influential for Jesus Christ.

Continued fellowship with God through the Holy Spirit opens up avenues of conversation that transform life. How fulfilling to converse with the God of the Universe! Our thoughts and feelings become more like those of God. Gaining God's perspective as He whispers words of life into our hearts brings incredible revelation. When God reveals Himself to us, we have plenty of opportunity to respond and make the most of each day. The choice to live each day as Jesus did is easier to make when we hear His voice lovingly directing and cheering us on.

The world we live in is filled with loneliness and emptiness. There are widows and orphans as well as the homeless and those who are destitute. Society includes millions of abandoned husbands and wives, brokenhearted and lonely, many of whom are single parents raising children. There are those who feel unloved, rejected, or unnoticed. Many Christians have distanced themselves from God while some don't know that fellowship with God is even possible. Fellowship with God is not only possible, it is essential. Even though the world is not a perfect place and we face the trials of life, we can take lasting comfort in fellowship with God. The apostle, Paul, praises God for His comfort to us in our suffering. *"Blessed be the God and Father of our Lord Jesus Christ, the Father of mercies and God of all comfort, who comforts us in all our tribulation"* (2 Corinthians 1:3, 4). For those who experience loneliness, rejection or distance from God, Jesus is the answer. Fellowship with Jesus through the Holy Spirit helps to overcome every difficulty. There is deep peace in the midst of all circumstances as only God can bring. Jesus left us with these familiar words from the Bible as a gift of peace to us. He said, *"Peace I leave you, My peace I give to you; not as the world gives do I give to you. Let not your heart be troubled, neither let it be afraid"* (John 14: 27).

God's presence is powerful. His power is there to protect, defend, and penetrate your life. Authentic, lasting peace will only come from God.

THE POWER WITHIN

The Power Within is pure
And opens the floodgates of heaven.
The Power Within tramples the adversaries of life.
The Power Within goes ahead and prepares the path,
That I will not stumble and fall.
The Power Within knows all things,
Prepares me for all things.
The Power Within loves me in the purest,
Most precious and everlasting fashion.
The Power Within rises up,
Protects, defends, and keeps me safe.
The Power Within is the presence of the Prince of Peace,
The only power and force in my life.

"O God, You are more awesome than Your holy places. The God of Israel is He who gives strength and power to His people. Blessed be God!" (Psalm 68: 35)

Communicating with God and spending time together deepens your relationship with Him. Think about your natural relationships with friends and family. You would have to agree that those you are closest to are the ones you spend the most time with. Genuine relationships develop over time. An infant has quantity time with his mother clinging to her for every need. Many children enjoy the friendship of a best friend every day. Adults who share interests and cross paths are more likely to become good friends. Family members that spend a good deal of time together tend to be very close. Jesus spent three years living with His twelve disciples, and they became intimate. In every genuine relationship there is a trust factor that rises up. Spending time together builds trust and strength in every relationship.

That is how it is with our Lord. When we spend time with God and work at communicating with Him, we are more likely to trust Him. Jesus is the perfect example of one who spent an immeasurable amount of time with the Father. If we follow in His footsteps, we will establish a trusting relationship with God.

Christians have the responsibility and great privilege of living within the will of God just as Jesus did. Jesus said, *"For I have come down from heaven, not to do My own will, but the will of Him who sent Me"* (John 6:38). When we do things God's way we are successful and please Him. Many of us struggle with everyday decisions because we have the willingness to do what God desires, but oftentimes we don't know what it is. It requires intimacy with God, and then the Holy Spirit gives advice in areas where we need direction or help. But understanding the will of God doesn't come at the snap of the fingers. We must cultivate our relationship with the Holy Spirit by renewing our minds daily to know God intimately. In Romans 12: 2, it says,

"And do not be conformed to this world, but be transformed by the renewing of your mind, that you may prove what is that good and acceptable and perfect will of God." Understanding the will of God comes by stepping out in faith, learning to listen for His will. How pleasing it is to God when we try! The voice of the Holy Spirit is refreshment to the weary soul. Knowing the will of God brings peace where quiet contentment is a delightful by-product. Adverse circumstances come along, but incredible peace carries those who listen to God and act upon His will. What a comfort to act upon the will of God instead of wandering in multiple directions! Think of how much we will accomplish for Christ; the list is endless.

Learning to communicate with God changes your prayer life. It is no longer a hopeless one way shout, but an open two-way system based upon mutual love and trust. When you go to prayer, you may boldly approach the throne of God and ask for His will concerning a specific need. *"Now this is the confidence that we have in Him, that if we ask anything according to His will, He hears us"* (1John 5:14). When we fine tune to the Holy Spirit, we hear what He has to say and pray accordingly. Sometimes the way we pray has nothing to do with God's plan. Oftentimes thoughts and emotions squeeze into the mind, and we tend to petition God according to the way we feel instead of according to His will. We repeat the same words aimlessly, hoping to persuade God. Prayer is exhausting when there are no words left to pray, and frustration sinks in when it appears God didn't meet the need. But prayer led by the Spirit is powerful, and much is accomplished on God's behalf. God's children are invigorated instead of burdened when they are led by the Holy Spirit, and prayer becomes a pleasure.

Allow the Holy Spirit to speak directly into your heart. Even one word from God is enough to penetrate your busiest day and set it apart as a holy day.

THE WHISPER

In the midst of the mighty rumble, the clanging noise
Is the sweet whisper of the One
Who loves me.
The One Who knows about the noises,
The rumbles of life.
Oh, the sweet, soft whisper…
More powerful than noise or an interference.
It will guide me and quiet the noise.
The whisper will bring peace to my soul
Like nothing else.
Listen for the whisper…soft.
Discover and follow the whisper,
For it is louder, more powerful
Than all the rumbles and noises of life.
The whisper blows over the mightiest rumble.
There is no power in the rumble, only in the whisper.
The whisper calls to me and says,
"Come and find peace!"

"But whoever listens to me will dwell safely, And will be secure, without fear of evil." (Proverbs 1: 33)

It is difficult to admit, but oftentimes I struggle to pray through my prayer request list every day. At times there seems to be no life in my list or in what I pray. Yet I know that prayer for others is essential, and we count on each other to carry our needs to the Father as Jesus did. Jesus must have had an enormous prayer list during His ministry. Still, He accomplished everything. How did He do it? Jesus told His disciples that He could nothing on His own; He had to consult with the Father to know the will of God in each circumstance. *"Then Jesus said to them, 'When you lift up the Son of Man, then you will know that I am He, and that I do nothing of Myself, but as My Father taught Me, I speak these things. And He who sent Me is with Me. The Father has not left Me alone, for I always do those things that please Him'"* (John 8: 28, 29). Jesus prayed perfect prayers according to what the Father instructed Him, and His prayers were always answered.

We may go to the Father as Jesus did and ask Him to direct our prayers concerning others. Then prayer becomes Spirit led, and the list comes back to life. Perhaps there is a strong leading to pray for certain ones, while others come to mind later on. Jesus was moved with compassion when He ministered. How incredible to operate with that same compassion when the Holy Spirit imparts a special desire to pray for certain ones! We actually **feel** their concerns. Moved by compassion, we boldly approach the throne of God on their behalf. The Holy Spirit speaks the will of God concerning what to pray, and prayers become more effective. A quiet peace comes when you pray the will of God and "just know" that your prayer is heard and that it is done. Answered prayer brings fulfillment and builds faith. It gives you the encouragement you need to continue to seek God for **His** will before sending your petitions to Him. Listening for God's voice and praying this way, opens the two-way communication system. It takes practice, but Jesus loves it when you look to His example and try your best to imitate Him.

My favorite part about hearing God's voice is simply enjoying **Him**! There are times when it feels like the Lord almost takes my breath away with His presence and sweet words of love. Even when I least expect to hear from God, He surprises me with words of love. I simply indulge in His loving kindness and truly feel like I am riding on top of the world. It brings praise to my heart, for nothing in life is better than that! *"Because Your loving kindness is better than life, my lips shall praise You"* (Psalm 63:3).

The Holy Spirit also whispers words of courage and strength to me when I am weak. My Creator tells me how wonderfully He made me to encourage and lift me up when my spirits are down. God takes an interest in the things that I do and meets me right where I am to bring wisdom and faithful instruction to my side. He knows that ultimately I will get to know Him better. When I am confused, the Holy Spirit whispers words of understanding so that I'll know what to do and give glory to God. In the Book of Ephesians in the Bible, Paul prays a beautiful prayer that encourages me to desire to know God and be filled with wisdom and understanding. *"...that the God of our Lord Jesus Christ, the Father of glory, may give to you the spirit of wisdom and revelation in the knowledge of Him"* (Ephesians 1:17). God desires to give wisdom and revelation to anyone who believes in Him.

The Lord's companionship infiltrates every aspect of life. He is real...real enough to experience and enjoy. When He speaks it is helpful to jot down every word to read for encouragement later. God becomes personal enough to reach out and touch. Don't be afraid that reaching for God will put Him on the human level, making Him a peer. That will not happen. A loving, personal relationship with God never takes anything away from Himself. I like to think about how Jesus related to His disciples. He enjoyed spending time with them. He was a friend to them, yet they had incredible respect and admiration for Him. Actually, when we relate to God this way, there is room for intimacy and a better understanding of Him. Intimacy gives rise to reverence and reverence for God keeps Him on the throne of all thrones.

There is no limit to the presence of God or what He has for you in that intimate place. Desire Him and see if God will not pour out an abundance of Himself just for you!

POUR FORTH

How blessed, to sit in your presence,
Basking in the light of Your glory!
I come to seek You; I shall not go home empty handed.
Indeed, I shall carry home box loads and crates
Filled with the light of Your glory.
When I seek You... earnestly, honestly, and truthfully,
I shall find You.
You lift me up and fill my vessels with everything about You,
More to give than I ask for.
Truly, I shall not limit myself; I speak of Your abundance.
I ask for all that I may have of You
That You will pour forth the light of Your glory
For I desire it so.

"Blessed is the man You choose, And cause to approach You, That he may dwell in Your courts. We shall be satisfied with the goodness of Your house." (Psalm 65:4)

Listening for the voice of God is a life long journey with exciting learning curves, mountains to climb, and some downhill paths to coast upon. It is like an adventuresome expedition in life when you keep your focus and fix your eyes upon Jesus. You know it is God's will for you to hear the voice of the Holy Spirit. Embrace His will, and work at listening daily. Perhaps there are some who may simply hear God without any kind of special effort or training. For me, that was not the case. Once I understood it is God's will for me to hear His voice, I decided to pursue Him and had to learn how to get to that secret place. My prayer life **had** to become a two way communication system. Knowing it is God's desire kept my intense pursuit of Him alive. Spending time reading my Bible and meditating upon scripture made me feel like I was on high potency, spiritual vitamins. It was a powerful way to strengthen my spirit and increase my desire to know God and hear from Him every day.

There were times when I wondered, is it really possible to converse with God? Whenever doubt crept in I spent extra time in my Bible, praying scriptures out loud that encouraged me to seek an intimate relationship with the Lord. God's Word is powerful! The more I read and spoke scriptures out loud, the less I doubted His willingness to fellowship with me. Life on the training ground did not stop there. I felt the Lord drawing me. In my spare time, for casual reading, I chose to read spiritual books and devotionals that would help to strengthen my spirit and listen for God. I continued to listen to uplifting Christian music and offered all of my praises unto the Lord. It wasn't long before I heard my first words from God. I was like a toddler taking his first steps to walk.

Remembering back, it was during a quiet time at a Bible study when I told God that I loved Him. Suddenly, it was as if someone wrote these words across my mind, "I love you too!" It is impossible to describe my feelings when I heard those words. I knew it was the Holy Spirit! Doubt surely could have overshadowed the moment that I had been waiting for, but I **chose** to exercise my faith and believe it was God. Small steps of faith are invaluable, especially when the mind tries to reason or contradict a feeling deep within. God knew how much I desired Him, and He was faithful. I knew that I **had** to believe it was God telling me that He loved me. Months of prayer had led up to that wonderful feeling, and it was like the "moment of truth" for me. Was I going to trust that The Lord had spoken to me or not? If not, perhaps it would have taken much longer to hear those profound words again. I believed, and it was enough to get me going.

Pursuing God's presence consumed my life. I developed a childlike expectation that I would hear from my loving Father again. More time in the Bible was essential to make my spirit stronger, yet sensitive to the voice of the Holy Spirit. Would I recognize the voice of the Holy Spirit when He spoke to me again? Some call it the "still, small voice within," while others told me that I would have a feeling or "just know" something. Only few Christians have heard God's voice audibly, but it can happen. God speaks through scripture, teachers, and anyone He chooses to use. The Holy Spirit speaks directly into the spirit; that is the still, small voice that many Christians describe. How would the Holy Spirit choose to speak to me the next time? Secretly, I hoped that God would speak just as He had when He told me that He loved me, and I prayed for that. The Bible says, *"And whatever things you ask in prayer, believing, you will receive"* (Matthew 21:22). I believe that everything the Bible teaches is truth, so I expected God to answer my prayer.

Thankfully, God answered my prayer, and the expected moment arrived. I was at a family gathering in the Rocky Mountains playing softball with my cousins and other relatives. Unfortunately, we had only one softball to play with. Someone hit the ball into the forest where it was lost, causing us to take a break from our game to search for the missing ball. We explored as much of the forest area as possible in desperate pursuit of the missing ball so that we could continue with our fun. After coming up short in our search, everyone decided to call it quits.

To my surprise the Lord spoke to me, and I was elated! It was more than the few words that I had expected. I heard the Holy Spirit tell me to secretly go back into the forest and wait for instructions. How faithful He was to meet me there in the midst of the dense woods! The Holy Spirit actually told me to take a certain number of steps, turn and go another few steps, and look down beside my feet. With excitement, I obeyed diligently and didn't feel a bit foolish. There beside my foot was the softball that we declared missing in action, never to return. I remembered jumping for joy in the forest because we could continue our game.

All at once, it hit me. The God of the Universe had just spoken to me and directed me into the woods to find the softball. My leap for joy lovingly turned into a reverent praise with head bowed and knees buried in the crusty leaves in the dirt. When I walked out of the forest tossing the ball in the air, my husband greeted me with a big smile. He suspected that God had spoken to me, and I was able to confirm his hunch with a satisfied smile. Perhaps, I had a look of amazement as if coming down from the Mount of Transfiguration. Truly, it was a life changing, mountain top experience for me! It confirmed my hunch that God wanted me to pursue Him personally and expect Him to meet with me.

Indeed, the Lord began to meet me. Most of the time conversation with God was only one way, but occasionally I heard His voice. I remembered, "Scripture is essential and practice is critical." Those words of wisdom were given to me by Chuck and Deb, the pastor and his wife who were spiritual mentors for my husband and me. Little did they know that those words would echo to encourage me on the training ground in the years ahead. I practiced by asking God all kinds of questions and then took little steps of faith in response. The Holy Spirit told me where to find certain scriptures in the Bible when I asked.

Talking and then listening was my goal on the practice field, allowing God to call the plays and direct my days. The Lord had permission to tell me what to do and when to do it. Eventually, God gave me creative dinner ideas and showed me how to alter recipes to please my family when I asked Him. Does God care about my family's dinner and major world issues at the same time? Yes, He absolutely does! The Lord knew that I was learning to hear from Him and that I desperately desired Him in every aspect of my life. God places no restrictions upon our prayer lives. He instructs us to simply ask of Him. In Matthew 7: 7-9, Jesus said, *"Ask and it will be given to you; seek, and you will find; knock and it will be opened to you. For everyone who asks receives, and he who seeks finds, and to him who knocks it will be opened. Or what man is there among you who, if his son asks for bread, will give him a stone?"* God has surely not given me a stone. The bread is fresh and soft and ever so satisfying because it is Him!

You are alive in Christ. You are like living water to a dry and thirsty world. You dazzle in the Son and your flow is steady and strong for all to see.

LIVING WATER

Living water...refreshing.
I delight in fresh, living water
Flowing down the mountainside.
Stop and listen to the gushing water,
The sound of purity, the glistening of the flow
As the sun shines upon the water to bring a sparkle.
A sprinkle, a few droplets from the water
Are refreshing to my dry, parched skin and lips.
Behold, the beauty and growth settle near the water
Where the soil is fertile, soft, and moist.
May I be like living waters, refreshing to my world,
Pure, alive, and glistening from the Son.
May I be an inspiration to others...
Set the flow for all to follow
And be as living waters.
And may I know where true living water is from,
To be all that I am to be.

"If anyone thirsts, let him come to Me and drink. He who believes in Me, as the Scripture has said, out of his heart will flow rivers of living water." (John 7: 37, 38)

The journey of listening and praying to God never ends. There's the excitement of the sharp learning curves and the ease of coasting downhill on some of the paths. Yet we must be prepared to climb a few mountains as well. There will be times when the Spirit of God may be silent. God might not always have something to say right when we desire for Him to speak. Waiting patiently can be difficult, trusting that God will speak when He knows we are ready for Him. When God speaks at critical times, choosing to believe it is Him can be challenging. Oftentimes the mind and emotions play havoc with each other, and the flesh speaks out to defy the promptings of the spirit. The will can be a stronghold mingling with distractions and influences of the world, causing confusion. Spiritual forces sneak through our cracks of weakness leaving a vulnerable spirit to defend. We must remember: *"You are of God, little children, and have overcome them, because He who is in you is greater than he that is in the world"* (1John 4: 4). Know that it **is** He who is in us, the Lord Himself, who graciously carries us up those mountain trails on the journey to hear His voice.

The Word of God is nourishment for your spirit, providing growth and maturity for the journey. Jesus said, *"It is written, 'Man should not live by bread alone, but by every word that proceeds from the mouth of God'"* (Matthew 4: 4). Study the Bible and remain grounded in the scriptures. Practice living with a heart of gratitude and praise unto the Lord. Intentional focus upon God clears the pathway, and the voice of the Holy Spirit becomes difficult to miss. Doubt and confusion give way to peace and understanding. Listening for small details leads to the knowledge of God's voice in the midst of difficult times and critical issues. Don't be afraid to try; it is a process, and God will meet you on your path no matter what speed you travel.

There are always adjustments to make along the way. The Spirit of God hovers with intensity to help everyone "fine tune" and hear His voice. It is part of the journey and becomes a way of life for those pursuing a relationship with God. God's peace is ever present to those who desire to know Him better. Don't be afraid to make a mistake when listening for the voice of the Holy Spirit. He is faithful. God desires fellowship with you more than you could possibly desire Him. In our family, we encourage one another when we talk about how difficult it is to misinterpret God's will when earnestly seeking Him. He is there for us. He opens our ears if we desire to have ears to hear. *"Sacrifice and offering You did not desire; My ears you have opened"* (Psalm 40:6).

Fellowship with God… doesn't it sound divine? Living in the presence of the Almighty…doesn't it seem heavenly? Yet it is a very realistic, earthly experience, and it is available to everyone now. Those who desire God and pursue Him faithfully will have true and lasting communion with the Holy Spirit right here on this earth.

"The grace of the Lord Jesus Christ, and the love of God, and the communion of the Holy Spirit be with you all. Amen" (2 Corinthians 13:14)

Three

TRUST IN GOD...Celebration of Dependence

I am Your child, innocent of transgressions
By the blood of Your Son.
Such comfort and peace
Established as Your very own.
Your very own, a part of You,
Partaking in everything of You.
Many choose to partake in the world
For it seems tangible to them.
To partake in You puts the world at my feet.
I am a conqueror, overcoming by Your Son,
Walking about with excitement and eager anticipation
As I depend upon You.
So I partake in You now,
And the world is at my feet.

CHILDREN ARE REFRESHING TO WATCH. The care-free attitude of a child is attractive to everyone. Seldom does a child skip along with worry tattooed across his face. What's there to worry about? Needs are met, and life is good. We were once like that; we were born that way. Remember when total dependency was instinctive, and needs were met upon demand? Unfortunately there are only a few flashbacks, but those precious images usher in feelings of security and comfort. Oh, to be like a little child again!

We **do** have the opportunity to be like little children again. Feelings of warmth and stability flow directly from the Heavenly Father to each of us because we are children in His kingdom. It is God's desire for us. In the Book of Matthew, when the disciples asked Jesus who the greatest in the Kingdom of Heaven was, Jesus answered. *"Assuredly, I say to you, unless you are converted and become as little children, you will by no means enter the Kingdom of Heaven"* (Matthew 18:3). Jesus knew that we must have that simple child-like trust and faith to depend upon our Heavenly Father for every need.

For many, dependency upon anyone is difficult. Maintaining a child-like attitude is a foreign thought. In our world, many strive for independence as a symbol of growth and stability. No one wants to be told what to do and especially not when. We've been conditioned to forgo the wisdom and authority of our parents and "stand on our own two feet" in a society that demands independence and self-reliance for survival. Certainly, we must grow and learn to make decisions and choices apart from our earthly parents. But it is always in our best interest to heed wisdom from their experience and years of counsel, regardless of our age. Mike and I have raised our children to grow and make wise choices of their own, knowing that one day they would live outside of our home. Yet as loving parents we are still available to them for counsel, emotional support, and encouragement as they venture out and explore the world for themselves. I shudder to think of our lives without the direction, support, and wisdom from those we know and love who have already made a few good marks on the pavement of life.

Jesus made the most significant, permanent mark on the pavement of life over two thousand years ago. He actually paved the road so that we can be like little children again, trusting and depending upon the parenting of our Heavenly Father. Jesus is the ultimate role model and the foundation for life now. His relationship with His Heavenly Father and dependency upon Him is a testimony to all of us. Looking at the life of Jesus, He epitomized the true meaning of dependency upon the Father in Heaven. He talked about how He could do nothing on His own. Jesus said, *"Most assuredly, I say to you, the Son can do nothing of Himself, but what He sees the Father do; for whatever He does, the Son also does in like manner"* (John 5:19).

Jesus lived a life of dependence upon God the Father. Again, He declares His reliance upon the Father when He says, *"I can of Myself do nothing"* (John 5:30). Why would the most perfect One of all time submit Himself to the Father? Surely as the Son of God, He was more than able to be self-sufficient. Jesus could have set a flawless example of independence for everyone to follow, but He didn't do that. God sent Jesus in human form to live a life that would go on record for us to imitate. Jesus was obedient to the Father and pleased Him; He was dependent upon God for everything. Jesus knew that submission to the Father results in lasting peace.

God eagerly waits for you to declare your dependence upon Him. He celebrates with joy every time you submit your will to Him, for He knows that you have everything to gain.

CHILDLIKE DEPENDENCE
May the excitement of my faith
Be contagious...
My childlike dependence bring joy
To Your heart.
You fulfill every desire and need.
Would you heal each wound and make
A sunny day for me?
It is not to question why or when,
Only submit to You, trust You.
Who would know Your timing?
Only that it shall be done by You!
Your Son walked in Your will,
Left the timing to You,
Concerned only for Your will.
You are my supernatural covering,
My All, my Everything.
Together we shall accomplish much
And I will gain so much from You!

"Teach me to do your will, For You are my God; Your Spirit is good. Lead me in the land of the uprightness." (Psalm 143: 10)

Trust God, turn your will over to the Father, and be obedient to Him; it is as simple as that! This is God's desire. God knows that when we do come to Him as children, willing to listen and live according to His purposes, His will can be accomplished. We are happier and much more content with life when we are in God's will. Yet what sounds simple isn't always easy. It takes genuine willingness to go against the flow of life, turn away from independence and acknowledge that apart from God, we can do nothing. The pleasure we bring to our heavenly Father is immeasurable. The peace we feel in a land of stress and strains is more refreshing than the cool splash of a waterfall on a summer day in the Rocky Mountains.

God's design is for us to be content and fulfilled every day. He doesn't place unrealistic expectations upon anyone. God doesn't rule from above, out of touch with reality. He created reality! He knows all about reality. Unfortunately, because of sin, our world is not perfect. Jesus said, *"These things I have spoken to you, trust in Me that you may have peace. In the world you will have tribulation; but be of good cheer, I have overcome the world"* (John 16:33).

Sin and trials naturally occur, and it was wise of Jesus to warn us of them through scripture. Yet His intent was not to bring fear and leave us feeling hopeless or dejected. Rather, Jesus spoke those words so that we are well informed and can take comfort knowing that He is there for us. We just need to depend upon Him. Our dependence upon the Lord is crucial. It is the answer to most questions about this fallen world that we live in. Depending upon God, waiting for Him, and living life on His terms might feel like squeezing through a narrow, rickety gate to walk the fine line on a treacherous path. Nothing could be further from the truth.

My brother-in-law, Chris, is a dedicated pastor and gave a profound message years ago that I recall. He said that the narrow pathway is the one that widens after you pass through the tiny gate, and it leads to the wide road of freedom. It is the broad gate and the wide road that eventually narrow and become almost impossible to stand and walk upon. They lead to bondage and destruction. What a dichotomy! Most look at it the opposite way. I like to think of the road to freedom as the road of total dependence upon God. The road to bondage is the road of independence and self-reliance. Which road will you choose? If you truly desire to live in the presence of God, the choice is not difficult to make.

The Holy Spirit is our Guide, and we are not forsaken in this world. Proverbs 28: 26 reads, *"He who trusts in his own heart is a fool, But whoever walks wisely will be delivered."* How marvelous to depend upon God's wisdom and to trust in Him! I take comfort in Psalm 32: 10 which reads, *"...he who trusts in the Lord, mercy shall surround him."* I want that for my life. Whenever I am fearful but rely upon myself, misery settles in, and it feels like I'm on the road to bondage. But when I stop and make the choice to rely on the Lord and trust Him, then the wide road of freedom is my path. I have incredible peace and hope that someone greater is at the control panel. That does not mean that there will always be instant gratification or that the problem is gone like magic. It only means that I am no longer in control and that my dependence upon the Lord brings peace and comfort as He works things out on my behalf. At times it seems miraculous and instantaneous, and other times there is a process that I must go through to trust God. *"And we know that all things work together for good to those who love God, to those who are the called according to His purpose"* (Romans 8:28).

How does a person practice dependence upon God in a culture that demands the opposite to achieve success and stability? Let's go back to the first two ingredients that help us to live in the presence of God. Remember God's sovereignty, keep Him upon the throne, and live in an attitude of gratitude. Understand and accept that all good things come from God. Practice humility, because life without need of God is futile. Acknowledge your need for Jesus and desire intimate fellowship with Him, and you can't help but trust Him for everything. Allow God to speak and listen tenaciously for the voice of the Holy Spirit. The reality of God through the voice of His Holy Spirit enables us to gravitate toward Him and desire His presence and leading, just as we crave the finest of foods. These first two ingredients are foundational in learning to trust God. Incorporate them, and God becomes real and trustworthy in your heart as well as in your mind. Dependency upon God naturally flows out of reverence and intimacy with Him.

Christians desire intimacy with God, but it takes practice and commitment to live in His presence. Those who are willing to submit to the Mighty Creator reap generous rewards. When I place my problems and concerns in His perfect hands instead of in my own stained and tainted hands, I am relieved. There are no words that describe the peace I have when I allow God to orchestrate each symphony of life and then take the final bow.

Peace is much more powerful and self-gratifying than any of the fake rewards that come from outside of God's presence and will. When I step out of the arena and give the credit to God, freedom is another step closer. When I choose not to struggle with burdens or agonize over decisions but turn them over to the Lord, the load is light. Jesus said, *"Take My yoke upon you and learn from Me, for I am gentle and lowly in heart and you will find rest for your souls. For my yoke is easy and My burden is light"* (Matthew 11: 29, 30). What an offer! Jesus desires for us to place our trust in Him because He knows how much better off we will be. God loves it when we trust and depend upon Him. He smiles upon our willingness to listen to Him and obey because we want to please Him.

Give God what rightfully belongs to Him... yourself, and allow Him to take control of your life. Experience His best.

TAKE CONTROL
You, O Lord, You are about trust.
My life trusts in You.
I am solely dependent upon You; I am at peace.
You are trustworthy; I have seen that in You.
Take control, my God!
I shall give it to You and let go of the desires
Of my flesh and my mind.
I lack nothing and thrive on Your existence.
Your provision shows in each area of my life
When I allow You to take control.
I trust in You,
In Your never failing love and character.
Take control, my God
That I may live the life You created for me.

"Blessed is the man who trusts in the Lord, and whose hope is the Lord. For he shall be like a tree planted by the waters, which spreads out its roots by the river, and will not fear when heat comes; but its leaf will be green."
(Jeremiah 17: 7, 8)

Drawing close to God is a lifetime practice. We know that He desires it; He created us for that purpose. Salvation and relationship with the Father through the Holy Spirit should be our first priority. Drawing close to God through intimate relationship transforms life for everyone. We become less reliant upon our imperfect ways and develop more of the character of God. Our son, Ryan, knows that true dependency upon God is critical for success in life. Once he wrote a note to us discussing God's will for us versus our will for life. He made a comment about the character of the apostle, Paul. Ryan wrote, "Paul's character was founded so deeply in the will of God that not even the fear of torture and death could persuade him to act out of selfish ambition." Paul spent a great deal of time with God in true submission to His flawless will; his new identity came from God. It is no wonder that he developed the character of God so beautifully.

The Lord will have His way in us when we have our identity in Him just as Paul did. Who could turn down the opportunity to be more like the most Perfect One of all time? When I realized that God wanted me to trust Him for everything and become more like Him, my life changed. Now I am passionate to pursue God and learn to live with Him on a moment by moment basis. God, in His loving compassion for us, sent Jesus to light the path and encourage everyone to pursue the Heavenly Father. We become more like our Role Model when we allow Him to draw us in an attitude of dependence and obedience upon God. Life becomes more of Him and less of ourselves when we practice trusting God and depending upon Him.

Reliance upon God produces an interesting result. The sinful obstacles of life diminish. The Bible says, *"Whoever abides in Him does not sin"* (1John 3:6). That is good news! You have received the gift of salvation through Jesus Christ, and He takes away the guilt and shame of sin. You are forgiven…period. Grace and mercy extend to you…period. Sin has no hold upon you. Simply walk in this knowledge, and you will draw close to God in total dependence upon Him. Sin attempts to creep in, but it is exposed by the Holy Spirit. The supernatural ability to slam the door on sin is there for you. Depend upon God, and make the choice to shut out sinful obstacles. When you fail and blow it, Christ is there. Repent, turn your back on sin again, and continue on the path of everlasting. *"Search me, O God, and know my heart; try me and know my anxieties; and see if there is any wicked way in me, and lead me in the way of everlasting"* (Psalm 139: 23, 24). What a perfect, little prayer before progressing on the journey!

I liken my journey with the Lord to a long road trip in the car. God is the dad, the driver, and I am His child in the back seat. He has the map and knows where we are going, where we'll stop to eat, and when we'll refuel. My Father knows what to do in heavy traffic and how to avoid dangerous accidents and unnecessary side roads that lead to frustrating dead-ends. In adverse weather, my Father has both hands steady upon the wheel, eyes peeled upon the road with an attitude of patience and control that puts me at ease in the back seat. Sometimes Dad chooses the most scenic routes enriching the trip and sights along the way. He is not often into short cuts. When I ask how much further, oftentimes my Father will lovingly remind His "back seat driver" that I don't need to be concerned about the final destination just yet. Dad lovingly tells His little girl to sit back, relax, and trust Him to get us there safely and on time. God's lead is perfect, and road trips like that are the best. Even when God takes the scenic route, He is always in control. Why not trust God and depend upon Him? Life is less worrisome, and stress won't have such a grip on you when you depend upon God and trust Him for everything.

In our culture, stress is a common word in almost every vocabulary. There is good and bad stress, funny and sad stress. There is emotional, physical, marital, and spiritual stress. I can add the word, stress, to any adjective and conjure up a new type of stress for any occasion. *"Be anxious for nothing, but in everything by prayer and supplication, with thanksgiving, let your requests be made known to God, and the peace of God, which surpasses all understanding, will guard your hearts and minds through Christ Jesus"* (Philippians 4: 6, 7). **In everything**, we are to submit our requests to God.

How many needs, wants, or stresses are there in a day? Surely there are enough to keep us in fellowship with God. Requests alone will keep us running to God moment by moment as part of living in His presence. When we place our needs before God with an attitude of gratitude and expect Him to take care of them, He will exceed every expectation. In the Bible, Jesus says that the Father will do great things for us. *"If you then, being evil, know how to give good gifts to your children, how much more will your Father who is in heaven give good gifts to those who ask Him"* (Matthew 7: 11). One of the most difficult things for me to do is trust and depend upon God while leaving my will and personal agenda out of it.

Once, I went through a time of learning to depend upon God for one of my most precious commodities, sleep. Generally, I can handle most issues as long as I've had enough sleep. Without a warning call from God, I slipped into a time frame of about two months when I was unable to get the proper sleep and rest that I needed. Each night I woke up after only a few, short hours of sleep, unable to fall back to sleep. Tossing and turning, watching the alarm clock tick away the hours of the night, I grew restless and uncomfortable. I tried all of the usual methods to get myself to fall asleep again. Surely if I get out my Bible, that will put me to sleep, I thought. After all, how many times do I fall asleep reading my Bible when I wish I hadn't? Oddly enough, I was able to read and gain incredible spiritual knowledge and insights but not sleep. I prayed for everyone I could think of without batting an eye. Television in the wee hours of the morning couldn't put me to sleep either. I even tried getting some work done, but that was not the solution. I only grew more tired. Because sleep is so precious to me, I would pray and beg God to allow me to sleep, but I still worked at it on my own with the usual methods each night.

I realized that in my efforts to get back to sleep, I was not at peace but even more restless and frustrated. My prayers went before the Lord, but I never stopped to ask Him **what**, if anything, He wanted me to do to get the sleep I needed desperately. I was busy asking for God's help, but I helped myself to restlessness instead. Was I really depending upon God? Realizing that I was dependent upon my own conventional methods, I regrouped and went back to the first step. "God, what do **You** want me to do?"

Thankfully, the Spirit of God lovingly impressed His desire upon my heart. The Holy Spirit told me to do nothing except lie still, trusting and expecting Him to help me sleep. How simple was that? I was actually embarrassed that I had gone to such great lengths without asking God what to do first. It felt peaceful to trust God for my precious sleep. I was able to sleep well once again. I do still wake up at times, but I try to remember to trust God to allow me to fall back to sleep in His arms. Sometimes my mind wanders far and wide, so I have to ask the Holy Spirit to direct my thoughts back to God. Oftentimes He will lead me to pray or meditate upon scripture. I always try to remain dependent upon God.

Dependency upon God is essential for every growing Christian. We can jump in there to make life happen on our own, or we can lie still when we need to and wait for God to speak. The Holy Spirit will give specific direction or He might say, "Trust Me and do nothing right now." Whatever He says, we can expect that an inner peace will come when we listen and obey God. Do you remember the peace that surpasses all understanding? It does guard your heart and mind through Christ Jesus!

Give God your burdens, and enter into that place of rest with Him. There is nothing you can do, but God will do everything for your benefit while you rest in His arms of hope.

STAY OF REST

Draw me, O Lord, may I enter Your rest?
My soul is worrisome, my faith tested.
I shall cling to You for my entrance to rest,
For great peace and renewal of faith.
I ask for provision, blessing and abundance.
Shall I receive it all in Your rest?
Make me mindful to watch for your blessings
In packages of bright colors... my name will be on the tag.
Make me patient, watching for
The fullness of Your blessings as I rest.
Surely they are on the way as I
Place my trust in You.
Blessings of joy, peace, and contentment,
These are provisions from You.
You love me, O Lord,
And You give me a perfect
Stay of rest in Your arms.

"Rest in the Lord and wait patiently for Him." (Psalm 37: 7)
"Therefore my heart is glad, and my glory rejoices; My flesh also will rest in hope." (Psalm 16: 9)

The Bible says, *"Trust in the Lord with all your heart and lean not on your own understanding; in all your ways acknowledge Him and He shall direct your paths"* (Proverbs 3:5, 6). We are level headed Christians seeking to do the will of God, aren't we? Then why can't we depend upon our **own** understanding? We forget that our sin nature plays a significant role in life. Each day is a battle between good and evil, and human life is naturally flawed with the infusion of sin. It seems natural to pick and choose when to trust God, depending on personal strengths and weaknesses. Yet trusting God is not a selective process. It is a lifestyle of total reliance, moment by moment, standing on the promises of the Bible. Those who live dependent upon God have a resolve to trust Him regardless of how they feel at the time. It is a choice to let go and trust God.

What is it about the trust factor that makes it so difficult to let go and let God take over? Oftentimes, we don't even know that we are not trusting God. We're busy speeding ahead and forget to seek Him. When we finally reach a peak of frustration, we remember that there is a higher source and frantically cry out to God. We were taught that we need to drum up mountains of faith in order to trust God. We don't want to admit that we are not good or strong enough to trust God or that we don't have quite enough faith to depend upon Him. It feels condemning because we see ourselves as Christian failures, since everything we are hinges upon our faith. We are not failures if we don't feel like we have the faith to move the mountains that the Bible talks about. Really, it begins with a simple willingness to admit weakness and a decision to trust and depend upon God.

A conversation with my son-in-law inspired me to trust God more. Jim was not yet married to our daughter when I told him how I admired his integrity in his relationship with her. He thanked me but admitted that he could never have done it in his own strength. Jim had to trust God and rely upon Him to make him the person that he needed to be in their relationship. The Holy Spirit took it from there. God spoke to the apostle, Paul, at a time of weakness. The Lord said *"My grace is sufficient for you, for My strength is made perfect in weakness"* (2 Corinthians 12: 9). It is better to allow a perfect God to turn weakness into strength than to try to do it alone.

Today's culture plasters expectations upon everyone to perform. Add the social pressures that weigh heavily upon us, and you will get another glimpse of why trust is so difficult to muster up. We are taught to do it ourselves, make it happen, and jump through hoops. Be self-reliant and depend upon no one; you can only trust yourself, right? Statistics reveal that broken relationships and marriages are rampant and that hurts and disappointments travel in greater magnitudes than ever before. Many are reluctant to trust anyone, afraid to be vulnerable. It seems far too painful. Pain builds upon pain, and life becomes unbearable. With defense mechanisms in place and walls of protection that block out intruders, we avoid hurt in any form and at all costs. How it must grieve our Father in Heaven, for He never designed it to be that way. God meant for it to be just the opposite. God wants us to have fellowship with one another and invest into the emotional and spiritual well being of others. In doing so, we are able to become transparent about our own lives with those whom we have true and lasting friendship. Within the safety of relationship we grow and learn to trust God and shed the weight of the world that we've been conditioned to carry.

Trust changes how we live and think. It rearranges priorities and stabilizes life. God intends for no one to be left alone. Everyone would self-destruct without trust because there is a built-in need for others and for God's intervention through those trusting relationships. Somehow, when we learn to trust others and feel secure, we are more open to trusting our Ultimate Source. That is the goal. Interestingly enough, when we work toward good relationships and become better at trusting God, those relationships blossom.

Life without dependence upon the Master's plan is dry, brittle, and selfish. Yet life in submission to the Father, yielding daily to His desire, is a life that is full, satisfied, and generous in every way. Some picture God as a tyrant, ranting and raving up in the heavens. They say God is busy taking things away from us to teach us worthwhile lessons. Sometimes we impose our perception of parenthood upon God the Father. Perhaps your parents were harsh, strict, not affirming, or taught lessons by encouraging failure and trouble.

Even though God might use difficult times to teach you, it is not in His character to withhold from you or be cruel. The Holy Spirit lives within you, always there looking out for your best interests. God sees things from an eternal perspective that sometimes we can't see for ourselves. He has the whole painting of life in mind and takes each stroke of the paintbrush seriously and precisely to create the masterpieces we were meant to be. If we would only give our personal canvass of abstract scribbling over to the Great Artist, we would be amazed at the lovely piece of work that we could become. It is our choice. The Holy Spirit is gracious and kind; He will not force anyone to do anything. We must choose to go against the natural flow of life and be stronger than the powerful current that will pull us under when we are not clinging to Jesus Christ. For those who cling to the Lord, the swim upstream is possible and well worth the effort to trust in God.

God's abundance not only provides, but it also protects and defends those who trust Him. The abundance of God breathes life and hope into every circumstance.

ABUNDANCE OF LIFE
Surely as I lift my eyes above,
I will find You
Above the rubble, destruction,
And imperfections of life.
You are waiting for your chosen ones
To call upon you and trust You.
For You know what might fall
And cause destruction.
Yet, You are there if I choose You!
Your Word is the abundance of Life.
Your death and resurrection, the abundance of life.
Your very presence today…
It is the abundance of life.
My choice is You.
Over the rubble, destruction, and imperfections…
I choose the Abundance of Life.

"You are my hiding place; You shall preserve me from troubles; You shall surround me with songs of deliverance."
(Psalm 32: 7)

I used to think that I had a pretty good idea about what it is like to trust God. The Lord knows that I have lots of growing to do in this area and began to teach me something new. When I wrote the beginning pages of this chapter I found myself praying, asking the Holy Spirit to bring words that would be meaningful. I desired to encourage His children to take steps of faith and trust Him. I even freed my calendar from chores for the summer so that I would have plenty of time to pray and write each morning. Surely God will speak to me, I thought. But the Holy Spirit was silent and that surprised me. I cried out to God again and again. "God you always speak to me, and I practice listening for your voice all of the time. Why are you silent now when I am counting on You to help me write this chapter?" There was no answer to my question.

It seemed meaningless to go on and try to do this alone. I filed away my pages and put my writing on hold. At first it felt like I was being disobedient to God's purpose for me. I felt guilty and lazy and thought perhaps I was being distracted by the excitement of the fun summer ahead. Did I have wrong motives? Was I unwilling to devote enough time to His will? Maybe I had been un-appointed and God had someone else to do His writing, I thought. Surely something was wrong with me as I failed to stay focused on my assignment, unable to hear from God.

Why was I thinking this way and where were these thoughts coming from? Eventually, I realized that those terrible thoughts and accusations could only come from our adversary, whose kingdom would love to destroy what God was doing through me. My loving Lord would never accuse me, nor would He cause me to feel that way about myself. God wants me to see myself as He does. I was obedient, and I had a strong willingness to serve God and run tenaciously to the finish line. It seemed logical to begin writing the chapter on trust. That was my logic, not God's. How funny that even though I was prepared and focused to serve Him with my writing, He had something else in mind! What I didn't realize is that the events of that summer would reveal His loving faithfulness to teach me more about what it means to trust Him. Looking back over the summer months, the Lord did just that!

Our daughter had just been engaged to be married. It was exciting, yet overwhelming as I contemplated all the work in the months ahead to prepare for her wedding day which would come in a year. Out for a walk one morning, I poured my heart out to the Lord. I reminded God that wedding planning is known to be stressful and that the responsibility would be more than I could handle. I had a panic attack right in the presence of God. I feared that the demanding busyness would take me away from writing this book.

The Holy Spirit was kind and spoke directly into my heart clearly. "Don't worry or be afraid; I will make this easy for you!" "Lord, is that really You," I asked? Was this the voice of God or just a comforting thought? In my spirit I knew it was God. It was my choice to trust Him and expect the preparation of the wedding to be easy. God is so good! In Philippians 4:19, the Bible says, *"And my God shall supply all your need according to His riches by Christ Jesus."* God **did** supply all of my needs, and He made it easy, just as He said He would do. My areas of concern were of no concern anymore. When I thought about difficulties ahead and began to fret, God brought just the right solution with little effort and kept the stress from bombarding me. The more that I decided to trust God, the more I could trust Him and the more I trusted Him, the more faithful I realized God is!

God is **always** faithful, but sometimes we don't notice or recognize His faithfulness. I began to take notice, for sure! The initial planning for our daughter's wedding came under quiet control that summer, and it was surprisingly effortless. It was a lot of work, but it didn't feel that way. It could have been a frazzling time, but thanks to the Lord it turned out to be a rewarding experience. By fall I was able to get back to writing, and I had spiritual experiences and valuable lessons to draw from.

How is it possible that wedding planning could become a spiritual matter? Was it only about God's goodness and kindness to me? I believe it was just a beginning, a way to get my attention off of my circumstances and onto the Lord who is more than able to care for any need or situation. There was a bigger picture. It was a valuable lesson for me in choosing to trust God for monumental details as well as trivial ones. God cared about my needs regardless of size. God took charge, and I witnessed His provision time and again over those summer months. I felt like I had great favor with God as He led me down the path without painful consequences. God's perfect faithfulness that summer encouraged me to begin to watch for Him in other seasons of my life as well.

Praise the Lord for your dependence upon Him. Praise His matchless ability to do exceedingly more for you than you could ever ask for.

TRUST IN YOU

O my Strength
You alone are capable of holding me up.
You overshadow and surround me.
You are sufficient;
My trust is in You.
There is no other source but You.
I will find all that is needed, in You.
You are my stronghold when trouble comes,
My hiding place...
My trust is in You.
Defend me from my enemies; keep them away.
Draw me closer, in love with You.
I depend upon You, my Strength,
My Stronghold, my Deliverer.
You will not forsake me
When I seek Your face.

"Now to Him who is able to keep you from stumbling, And to present you faultless before the presence of His glory with exceeding joy, To God our Savior, Who alone is wise, Be glory and majesty, Dominion and power, both now and forever. Amen." (Jude 24, 25)

Life is full of ups and downs. There are mountain top experiences and valley happenings. Jesus didn't promise only mountain top joys. In fact He said, *"In this world you will have tribulation; but be of good cheer, I have overcome the world"* (John 16:33). Everyone has personal issues, rubbish to work on, and baggage to unload. We can take on the burdens of life or raise our arms to the Lord for help. Issues with others tug heavily upon the heart. We can be self-righteous or lay down pride and allow God to work wonders. It doesn't matter what the obstacle is; we can rely on God.

The challenge to move forward and depend upon God will always be there but that's the beauty of the Holy Spirit; He's raring to go. Stress and worry diminish with the intervention of God's Spirit. Prayer takes on a new dimension because in asking we also choose to **learn** to trust God for an answer in His way and timing. Learning to trust God through prayer is a helpful exercise since we are all yearning to "arrive." God wants to capture us and take us places we've never been in the learning process to trust Him. Life is a wild ride with difficulties, but the bumps and pot holes are manageable with the Holy Spirit at the helm. Everyone who seeks God arrives safely.

It is my prayer that you will be encouraged to take a step of faith and believe that if the God of the Universe would show His faithfulness and trustworthiness to me, then He will reveal it to you as well. Ask God for a revelation of His faithfulness, but be realistic and expect that you will have to take a step of faith to trust Him. Listen for God's voice, expect to hear it and then live in an attitude of gratitude toward Him. God's ways always amaze me. I rejoice in my helplessness because He is creative and always by my side. In His faithfulness, God is more than able when we are willing to lay it all down and depend upon Him.

Each day life reminds me that freedom is one of our most cherished possessions. We sing songs and read literature about freedom. We display flags and stickers and see billboards with famous quotes about freedom. Goose bumps rub against my sleeves at the sound of songs of patriotism and of our nation's freedom. Hair stands on end at a glimpse of the Statue of Liberty and its significance. Freedom is not to be taken for granted. Thankfully we have freedom in Jesus Christ, and that is nothing to be taken for granted either. Jesus freed us from the consequence of sin and has given us access to the Kingdom of Heaven as a gift of our salvation.

If you had the opportunity to visit God in Heaven for a day, you would go in a heartbeat. Yet God has given you the ability to access everything about Him, through Jesus Christ, right here on earth. Will you pursue Him? God requires you to trust Him and walk down the path which leads to freedom in this life. What a fulfilling way to live! You no longer have to trust yourself. Your trust is in the Holy Spirit that lives within you, and you learn to live in the presence of God. When we are led by His Spirit we have liberty. Depending upon God and trusting in Him **is freedom** at its best!

"Now the Lord is the Spirit; and where the Spirit of the Lord is, there is liberty." (2Corinthians 3:17)

Four

DESIRE FOR GOD...Heart's Desire

Early in the morning I see the reflection of the sun
Against the backdrop of the sky and clouds.
So it is with You!
I see You and Your reflection against any backdrop of life.
And I want to be a lovely reflection of You in any backdrop,
Scene or circumstance.
When I saw the reflection of the rising sun this morning
There was such beauty.
But in Your reflection against the sky of life, I am speechless!
There are no words great enough to describe what I see.
May I shine as You do,
That all will see brilliant Son-shine,
Visible and reflective in my life.
May You be visible to all who look and gaze and admire
The Son in every backdrop of life.

Isn't it fun to be a winner? Most of us have been on the receiving end and know the feeling. Perhaps it was a door prize, and your name was picked. Maybe you were chosen in the lucky draw or had the matching number. Regardless of the prize, it feels good to win, and it does wonders for your morale. I've yet to see a winner without the silly grin that says it all. Yet Christians wear that same winning smile, but not by the luck of the draw or random chance. They are the ones who have accepted God's invitation for salvation, and Jesus is their precious prize. They have cashed in on life, and they are on the receiving end of God's goodness.

The irresistible charm and character of Jesus has been awarded to you. What a prize, much more than you could ever hope to have! You have Jesus, and His matchless ability to love with no limitations now belongs to you. All you have to do is bring Him home to your heart forever. It is a "button bursting" experience as God takes up residence there. You might want to clear out the clutter in a special room of your heart to make prime space for Jesus. Perhaps you could even take a crash course on interior design and decorate that room to make it aglow so that our Lord is comfortable residing there. Picture that, a room with a view within your heart so desirable that the Holy Spirit of the Living God would establish permanent residency. Human nature tempts us to de-clutter and redecorate before bringing home our most Prized Possession. But Jesus says that we are desirable to God just the way we are.

God finds the humble abode of your heart to be the perfect, cozy bungalow from where He will have great intimacy and fellowship with you. The Holy Spirit inhabits your whole heart, not just an attractive corner that has been redecorated for God. When you asked Jesus to be the Lord of your life, you became a member of God's household joined to Him by Jesus Christ. You live in Christ, and Christ lives in you. Nothing you can do will make you more desirable to the Father. Actually, the Lord wants us to desire **Him**. Everything about Him is desirable; everything is excellent. God makes Himself irresistible to His children through His Word and His Spirit so that we will desire Him and all of His attributes. The Lord is our desire, our delight. There is nothing in Heaven or on earth more attractive than our Lord. *"Whom have I in heaven but You? And there is none upon earth that I desire besides You"* (Psalm 73: 25).

When Jesus becomes the desire of your heart, you become teachable and open to transformation so that you can live with God, moment by moment. It is what you long for, isn't it? It is the reason that you are reading this book. You long to spend each moment in the presence of the Holy Spirit, but you are not going to get yourself there by coincidence. It doesn't just happen; you must purpose to live with God and desire what He is all about. Your nature will change and God's attributes become yours when you desire Him so.

When we practice trusting God and depend on Him for everything, we share in His character. We find God to be as trustworthy as Jesus did. Life is more peaceful when trusting God. No one has a better sense for what is best for you than God does. Certainly you and I won't make a better decision or judgment call on our own. The more completely we depend upon the Holy Spirit to guide us in every way, the more we will desire God and aspire to be like Him. Imagine longing for God moment by moment, preferring His nature and will over yours. Some would say that steals the freedom we were given and zaps the excitement out of life. After all, didn't God create us with a free will to make choices and decisions on our own? Shouldn't we be the ones calling the shots? Others would say that good deeds and godly desires are simply the result of trial and error, not because of a submissive heart to God. Still others think that we can desire the good things that Jesus taught us but that having a desire and passion for the **person** of Jesus Christ is not realistic. None of this is true. The Bible makes it very clear that God wants us to desire Him.

Certainly every Christian has the choice to follow God's way after hearing the Holy Spirit speak the will of the Father. The Holy Spirit never forces anyone to accept God's way; it is always a personal choice. Life presents us with a double measure of adventure when operating within God's plan. It is pleasing to God when we don't mutter through our fragmented, imperfect thoughts in the decision process. The Holy Spirit gives a much broader prospective with more thought provoking and prayerful considerations to choose from than we can conjure up on our own.

If we desire God then we must want all of Him, even His characteristics. Oftentimes in prayer, we express the desire to learn more about God's wisdom, knowledge, and understanding; we ask Him to teach us to operate with His character. What an education! There is no college curriculum on earth that is capable of teaching or competing with what God imparts. Think of all God must have taught Solomon in granting his prayer request to operate with His wisdom. Imagine how much you will learn from God when you ask Him for the knowledge and understanding to sift through the difficulties of life, just as He would. This deep desire is foundational because it keeps the focus on God. The goal is not to **be** God or attain all He has. The goal is the process of listening, trusting, acting, and then believing that we are growing close to God, living in His presence.

God is more than able; He is the only one who can satisfy your deepest longing. His presence is the real thing, and no phony substitute will measure up to God.

SATISFY MY DESIRE

You have given me a taste of life in Your presence.
Now I hunger more; will You satisfy Me every minute
Of each day?
Your sustenance is flavorful, full bodied, and rich
In the nutrients of life.
I will go deeper and desire You more,
And You will satisfy my desire with Your presence.
Still, my desire for You grows.
You give unto me and I nurture, hold, and treasure each
Moment with You.
I will never grow tired of You; I will always desire You.
My love for You is real, not a story or a myth to tell about.
It comes from a desire to have intimacy with You,
To have access to You, needing and wanting more.
I will speak of the truth, of abundant life in Your presence.

"Oh, that men would give thanks to the Lord for His goodness, And for the wonderful works to the children of men! For He satisfies the longing soul, And fills the hungry soul with goodness." (Psalm 107: 8, 9)

Sitting under the Lord's leadership and training, we experience Him at a deeper level. We ask; He answers. Sometimes we misinterpret what the Holy Spirit has to say when we toss a bit of our will into the listening process. This is common because we are not God. We are disciples, learning, experiencing, and trying our best to do it His way. In fellowship with the Holy Spirit and with God's mercy and grace, we re-group when mistakes are made and go back and learn to listen again. The Holy Spirit is always there for guidance.

Oftentimes, we go forward assuming that the little tip of guidance we got from God is enough to turn over the engine and send us merrily down the path. We have our own road maps and can figure it out from there, right? Yet frequently we get a short way down the path, come to a fork in the road, and wish we had a little more Godly insight to know which way to go. God doesn't fret about that. Instead, His grace and mercy is freely extended when we acknowledge our mistake and ask for His help. We let go of our self-righteous pride, seek God's plan, and start back on the path again.

Quite often, by the time we get to that fork in the road we are too full of pride, and we don't think to ask God for direction. Sometimes we find ourselves at a dangerous dead end or on the edge of a cliff and get angry with God. We tend to blame Him for not covering our tracks. "Lord, Lord, where were You? Why didn't You intervene? I could have gone over the cliff!" Does that sound familiar to you? Guess what? God was there, waiting for that desperate plea for help. Even when we choose a difficult or destructive path, we can turn around and God's forgiveness covers those prideful trails. Does that sound like a God you can desire every minute? It is the Lord's will for us to cry out and acknowledge our need and desire for Him. It's all a process but the Holy Spirit is faithful and patient if we proceed with Him and not without Him.

"He who calls is faithful" (1 Thessalonians 5:24). The Lord never misses a beat, is never late, nor does He ignore His precious ones whom He has called. This includes you and me. In 2Peter 3:9, Simon Peter talks about how God desires that no one should perish but that all should repent and have eternal life. We are all called into the Lord's kingdom to experience His faithfulness. God wants us to share in another part of His character, His great faithfulness. Once we have had a taste of God's faithfulness, we can believe for more. David wrote in Psalm 34: 8, *"Oh taste and see that the Lord is good."* God's faithfulness reaches to the highest peaks as well as the deepest plummet imaginable. He is there; all we have to do is take a step of faith and ask for an abundance of His faithfulness. It is an integral part of desiring God and all that He is. Then the really wonderful part comes. Our Savior imparts His faithfulness back to us. We can walk in the same faithfulness that Jesus modeled when He lived on the earth. We'll have that same irresistible demeanor that Jesus had. Those who approached Jesus knew He was there for them. They desired what Jesus had to offer, and He was always faithful to give. Do you want your life to reflect the faithfulness of God? What an honor to be considered faithful just as Jesus is faithful!

God's faithfulness is manifested in your life everyday. Watch for Him; experience the Lord in the simple things, and grow to recognize His faithfulness in the complexities ahead.

PERFECT FAITHFULNESS

You, O Lord, are Perfect Faithfulness.
I come in honesty and humility, and I see Your faithfulness.
You would turn Yourself inside and out that I would see You.
Many only look to Your works and deeds, but I will not.
*I don't long for Your perfect performance, I desire **You** and who You are.*
When I experience You, I feel Your faithfulness.
How simplistic!
I shall desire only You…I have everything I need.
My passion for You grows.
I will stop at nothing in my pursuit of You,
And Your perfect faithfulness will shine before me.

"Through the Lord's mercies we are not consumed, Because His compassions fail not. They are new every morning; Great is Your faithfulness. "The Lord is my portion," says my soul, "Therefore I hope in Him!" (Lamentations 3: 22-24)

Living faithfully as Jesus did means having a heart of obedience. The greatest act of obedience of all time is recorded in the Bible. In the Garden of Gethsemane, Jesus experienced great sorrow and cried out to the Father in agony. Jesus knew the will of the Father and that He had to suffer death on the cross for our sins. Yet Jesus made the choice to be obedient even unto death. *"O My Father, if it is possible, let this cup pass from Me; nevertheless, not as I will, but as You will"* (Matthew 26:39). Knowing God's will and acting upon it go hand in hand. The Holy Spirit imparts God's will, but it is up to you to carry it out according to God's plan. Your heart must be open to the Holy Spirit. Always listen for direction with an attitude of obedience, and be wise to put the will of God into action according to His plan. When you listen to the Holy Spirit and use wisdom to obey, then the Father is pleased and able to use you for His purpose in His kingdom on earth. This will carry you another step closer to living in His presence.

You might be wondering if the Holy Spirit will speak to you or if you are even able to hear His voice as we discussed in chapter three. It is helpful to remember that the Holy Spirit enjoys speaking. His voice resounds deep within your heart. He speaks through the Scriptures, other people, and circumstances in life as well. As you learn to recognize God's voice and obey faithfully, you are operating with the same integrity as Jesus, steadfast to the finish. It is gratifying to know you have accomplished something for God no matter how insignificant it might seem. The desire to go above and beyond a mediocre lifestyle, seeking after the Lord and His ways, becomes insatiable. The more obedient you become, the more God will use you and the more of Him you will desire.

We become compatible with the Living God as we live out our faith in His footsteps and in His presence. Walking in the footsteps of Christ, we sense something uniquely warm in the character of His footprint. His deep compassion for all of mankind oozes out every time our Lord generously takes a step on our behalf. Our Loving Savior actually feels what we feel; He shares in our humanity. When Jesus showed compassion to the hurting, He felt the same pain and sorrow as they did. I marvel at the story in the Bible of Lazarus and how Jesus loved him and raised him from the dead after being in a tomb four days. It is a moving account of love and compassion intertwined with the miraculous power of God.

In the book of John we read of Lazarus, the brother of Martha and Mary, who was very sick. His sisters sent for Jesus in good faith that He would come and heal their brother. Yet Jesus did not go to them until after Lazarus had died. When Jesus approached their town, Martha ran out to meet Him, pouring her heart out to Him. In great faith, Martha believed Jesus when He told her that Lazarus would rise again. When Mary and the other Jews came to where Jesus was, Mary cried out, weeping at the feet of Jesus. *"Therefore when Jesus saw her weeping, and the Jews who came with her weeping, He groaned in the spirit and was troubled. And He said, 'Where have you laid him?' They said to Him, 'Lord come and see.' Jesus wept. Then the Jews said, 'See how He loved Him'"* (John 11:33-36). The story ends when Jesus calls out to Lazarus to come forth from the tomb. Lazarus is raised from the dead!

What a powerful account of miraculous compassion! Jesus felt their pain and moved with compassion to bring Lazarus back to life. Did Jesus raise Lazarus from the dead because of His love for him or because He loved the others and felt their pain? Jesus felt many emotions that day, and He responded to each of them. That is what I desire to do. It is my hope and prayer that the Lord will bless you and me with the same measure of compassion that brought the miraculous to the forefront of life. We might not all be raising people from the dead, but we may all share in the same compassionate heart of Jesus and act on His behalf everyday. That would be a powerful miracle in itself. A little compassion goes a long way, but a lot of compassion could change the world. Jesus did!

The Lord is compassionate and bestows mercy and forgiveness to all who ask for it. We all blow it. We make mistakes, and we definitely sin. None of us enjoys regrets or the pain involved with failure. How marvelous to know that by the power of the blood of Jesus, through His death and resurrection, we don't have to live with guilt or regret! Jesus died for every sin and regret, rising from the dead to free each one from the bondage of sin. We are forgiven because we belong to Jesus, and our sins and failures are forgotten forever. What a powerful act of mercy, an attribute of God to be desired and treasured forever! *"Oh give thanks to the lord, for He is good! For His mercy endures forever"* (Psalm 36:1).

God's mercy is never ending, yet it is the happy ending to failure and sin. It penetrates into the darkest crevice of the heart and destroys guilt and shame. Mercy is essential. None of us will grow and mature in the Lord to reach that place of true intimacy with Him without mercy and forgiveness. If we choose to withhold mercy and forgiveness, we will drive a sharp wedge between ourselves and God. That wedge lodges within those deep areas where we have not extended pardon and pierces our ability to relate to God freely. Since we desire to live in the presence of God, we must be able to relate to Him so we can flourish in His will. Yet we won't flourish with the Lord if we don't practice forgiveness toward others or refuse to extend a hand of grace and mercy when it is needed. Allow yourself to freely receive God's mercy, and you will freely forgive. In Matthew 10:8 Jesus says, *"Freely you have received, freely give."* Whatever God gives to you must be given to others as well. How do I know if I have truly forgiven my brother or sister, you might ask?

Forgiveness is a choice, but sometimes it can be difficult. Your mind might say that you have done your duty to forgive, but you might still be at odds within your heart. What do you do now? There is not enough strength and fortitude to forgive on your own; it takes God's Spirit and love. Make the choice to forgive and then ask God to empower it. God's love always brings healing and peace when forgiveness and mercy are genuine. God's peace is the deciding factor when your mind and heart are at war with one another. Pray for God's peace as you strive to live in mercy and forgiveness. *"…and the peace of God, which surpasses all understanding, will guard your hearts and minds through Christ Jesus"* (Philippians 4:7). The Bible says that whatever you sow you will also reap; so then be merciful unto others. In the beloved Beatitudes Jesus said, *"Blessed are the merciful, For they shall obtain mercy"* (Matthew 5:7).

The Greatest Person of all time…what was it about Him that stands out most in a crowd and endured the test of time? Actually, everything about Jesus is elevated and exulted; He is irresistible. But the extravagant love of Jesus is abundant and reaches out to everyone. His love continues to withstand the test of time. Jesus said, *"As the Father loved me, I also have loved you; abide in My love. This is my commandment that you love one another as I have loved you"* (John 15:9, 12). We must desire the same love that Jesus has for each of us. It is His commandment to all of us who believe in Him.

The love of Jesus is deep, so divine that it impacted the world like nothing else has ever done. Jesus brought love into the world and overcame evil and hate with it. He led the battle for freedom with unselfish love. Jesus poured His love out to the unlovable and to the untouchables. He taught some of the Jewish leaders from the Bible what it means to love. Jesus radiates warmth as the author of unconditional love. We were born with a sin nature; unfortunately nobody has to teach us how to sin or disobey God, it just happens. The perfect love of Jesus Christ covers every one of those sins so that we won't reap the consequence of failure. Jesus loved so perfectly that He even conquered death with love. His life on earth is the flawless representation of the kind of love that the Father desires each of us to have.

We have all experienced love in some way. We were loved the moment we entered this world as infants, no matter what might have happened after that. Everyone extends love in some form. We know that warm fuzzy feeling, but it is impossible to describe how we know we love…we just do. But what about the love that goes beyond feeling? There is a deeper kind of love that rises when circumstances keep us from feeling the warmth of love. Jesus exemplified this type of love, unconditional and unselfish. It has no boundaries, and it cannot be measured. The love of Jesus fought every battle and won every cause.

Learning to love without additions, subtractions, or expectations is essential. The perfect love of Jesus is on the brink of your heart, ready to explode in your spirit and penetrate your life.

INNOCENT LOVE

Dear Lord, there is no substitute for You and Your presence.
And yet You tell me that there is no substitute for my love.
Many will work to gain Your acceptance,
Your approval, and even Your favor.
But I will simply love and desire You
With complete innocence, sensitive to Your Spirit.
Then I shall have Your acceptance,
Your approval, and even Your favor.
From innocent love comes obedience, perseverance, patience,
And Your Godly character.
No wonder love is the greatest gift!
I know that You cherish my heart of love
And I shall enter into Your presence.
Yes, You cherish my heart of love.

"Like an apple tree among the trees of the woods, So is my beloved among the sons. I sat down in his shade with great delight, And his fruit was sweet to my taste. He brought me to the banqueting house, And his banner over me was love."
(Song of Solomon 2:3,4)

There was a time when I really struggled with a particular issue and found myself in a battle, unwilling to succumb. It didn't feel right to surrender, and I couldn't muster up the feelings to forgive. I had been treated unfairly again and again. I needed to be sure it didn't happen anymore. My lips were pursed, my arms were folded, and I refused to allow my pride to budge. I wanted victory for myself, and I was ready to go for it. My pride had been hanging out on the line to dry, and the wind had blown in a storm that wreaked havoc with the stubbornness of it. This was my cause, and it was a noble one. My self-righteousness would ride on the front battle line on my behalf. Self mattered most of all, and because of that I was prepared to fight.

I got on my "high horse," my defenses were up, and I was prepared for victory. Amazingly, I remembered to get off of my horse for just a moment, bend a knee, and bow my head in prayer before I headed out to battle. As I remounted my "high horse" and rode off, I felt certain that God would be on my side. The Holy Spirit spoke to me and said, "Don't you know that you are prepared to lose? You will cause hurt and devastation if you go out to battle that way." Then God spoke through the Holy Spirit and said one of the most profound things that I have ever heard. It was a simple sentence that changed my plan of attack and then my life.

God said, "Battles are fought with blood, but truly they are won with love!" That was enough to bring my battle horse to a dust-cloud of a stop so abruptly that I almost fell to the ground. Instead, I got off my "high horse" and hit the ground of my own accord, planting my face in the dirt and cried for forgiveness. That day I asked the Lord to teach me more about His love.

The dictionary has several definitions for love, all of which imply feeling. Yet love is not merely a feeling; it is an act of the will. It is a conscious decision and a firm stance that says that I choose to extend love no matter what. It doesn't matter if love is returned to me or not. Most of us know this, but it is difficult to appropriate. We struggle because it is not our natural tendency to love as the Bible instructs. In the Bible the apostle, Paul, defines love as it should be. *"Love suffers long and is kind; does not seek its own, it not provoked, thinks no evil; does not rejoice in iniquity, but rejoices in the truth; bears all things, believes all things, hopes all things, endures all things"* (1Corinthians 13: 4-7). When I close my eyes and meditate on those inspired words I realize that so often I operate out of feeling instead of out of what is true about love.

"It is impossible to love like this all of the time, God, that is too tall of an order for me," I prayed. Maybe those words from the Bible were for Paul and the Corinthian people of that time period. Then the Holy Spirit reminded me that either all the principles of the Bible are true for today, or none of them are. No one has the ability or the authority to pick and choose out of the Bible. I had to make a choice to love as the Bible instructs. "God, that is still too tall of an order for me." The Holy Spirit agreed that it is too much for me to conquer on my own, but He lovingly offered to fill the order for me. God's overwhelming love brought me to tears. I sent my request to God and asked Him to teach me to love His way. I sealed it with a promise to be the best student I could be if He would help.

When we admit that we cannot, but with God we can, we are open to miracles of renovation within the heart. The love in

1 Corinthians is attainable and might look something like this... The Holy Spirit will lovingly remind us to stop and respond to difficult situations with patience and kindness. Without the slightest bit of jealousy, we are able to rejoice with those who attain what we'd like to have. We won't feel the need to attach our names on the tag of every good deed, looking for praise and recognition. We won't have the bench mark on life that entitles us to hefty royalties or anything we want. Won't it be rewarding to keep quiet, be a good listener, and then speak the truth in love without hurting others? Perhaps we might look out for others more than ourselves. What a blessing to learn to process anger and respond with words and actions that restore instead of destroy! The tally sheet that records offenses will find itself crumpled up in the trash bin. Our delight will be in righteousness and justice, rejoicing when truth comes to the forefront. God will teach you how to hold on to what is yours, but only with a light grasp. Each day you will trust God, knowing everything belongs to Him and that He is always in control. Precious hope rises when you fix your eyes on Jesus and pour all of your doubts down the drain. Yes, you will run the race with supernatural endurance, focused on Jesus. God's love becomes **your** love, never failing.

If it all sounds good to you but seems like an unrealistic dream, keep in mind that every one of us is a work in progress and that this is your journey. If your focus is on the love of Christ then you won't have to **force** yourself to love in a Biblical way. You won't need to make a gigantic list of what love is and then wear yourself out trying to conquer and capture each love item on the list one by one. The love of Christ will flow naturally.

The Holy Spirit does the work of changing you from the inside out so beautifully that you won't feel the need to take the credit. Instead, with great joy you will wholeheartedly give the glory and thanks to God, as it should be.

You will find yourself saying and doing things like Jesus did and wonder how that happened. Surely God must have intervened because I noticed how patient I was waiting in line at the grocery store, even though I would be late for my next appointment. I know I was the righteous one in that conversation with my husband, but how is it that I allowed him to be right this time, and it didn't even frustrate me? My schedule was totally disrupted due to the needs of others, but somehow it didn't matter that I made no progress today on my list of things to do. Where did all that kindness and love come from? It wasn't on my list to conquer today! The genuine love of Christ is naturally supernatural, and you are astounded at your change of attitude and your treatment of others.

We press in on this journey, seeking the character of Jesus Christ with assurance that His Spirit does live within us to guide and transform us into more of what we desire to be. Our goal is to be more like Jesus and live in the presence of God. We make mistakes, but thank God for His grace and mercy. There is never any condemnation when we fail and then remember to ask for forgiveness and help. In Philippians 4:13, 14, Paul inspires us to continue on. *"Brethren, I do not count myself to have apprehended, but one thing I do, forgetting those things which are behind and reaching forward to those things which are ahead, I press toward the goal for the prize of the upward call of God in Christ Jesus."*

You will encounter God only when you desire Him. He will not force Himself upon anyone. Ask for more of God, and He will delight in making Himself available to you. Perfection isn't what God desires. God only wants you to love Him and be near Him. Our daughter, Amber, had been praying, asking God to be the true desire of her heart. She sent me a happy birthday email which encouraged me to desire God and realize how lovely He is. Amber wrote, "God really is altogether lovely and desirable; He is wonderful. He has all the attributes we could want in someone whom we love and who loves us. This shows me that because He is so desirable, wonderful and lovely, He is so worthy of my praise everyday." Giving praise to God everyday is exactly what we have the privilege of doing. The more of God we desire, the more of Him we'll have. Will we ever have enough of our Lord?

Mike has always encouraged our children and me to desire all of God that we can. He uses the example of a buffet feast where the food is all too appetizing. He tells us to go to that buffet everyday and fill the biggest plate we can find with as much of God as we can pile onto it. He warns us not to take a small, side dish plate because we won't get full or be satisfied with just a small portion of Him. There is no limit to how much of God we may have. There is always more of God to desire. Thanks to my husband's revealing analogy, I even like to think about going before God each day with my biggest plate and an oversized platter to replenish my plate. Then I ask God to fill all of my vessels and containers until they overflow. During difficult times and periods of trial, we can sit before the Lord and eat and drink all of Him that we want. We all love the Twenty-third Psalm. It is what I call the "calm me down psalm." *"You prepare a table before me in the presence of my enemies; You anoint my head with oil; My cup runs over"* (Psalm 23:5). How about getting our bathtubs out for the Holy Spirit to fill? Then we can relax and soak in all of Him for as long as we desire. I know that I rest much better when I have had a soothing, Holy Spirit bath after a stressful day! The most important thing to remember is that the Lord is there for you. The Holy Spirit is accessible, and you can have all of Him that you desire.

Is it only a feel good experience that we heap onto our platters, or is there something tangible for us to grasp with an assurance of God's presence and indwelling? Really, it is a lot of both. When I pile on as much of the Lord that I can on my plate, there's plenty of the tangible to take in. There is an abundance of scripture to read and meditate on all day. There is always a gigantic helping of praise and worship to enjoy. Prayer and fellowship with God make a perfect blend of flavors on the plate. Then comes the rich sauce or seasoning that we pour on the top of the plate to add just the right touch. Perhaps it is a visit or a meal to someone who is not feeling well or a word of blessing to the discouraged. It could be a hug, a smile, or an affirming pat on the shoulder. Maybe it is a donation of time or finances to a needy cause or ministry. Friends offered their mountain town home to us for a weekend of refreshment during a tiresome season. Their generosity ministered mounds of flavorful toppings on our plates. The varieties and the portions of God that go onto our plates each day are not perishable, and they are endless. God is endless and what He has for us has no limitations. Jesus said,

"Do not labor for the food which perishes, but for the food that endures to everlasting life, which the Son of Man will give you, because God the Father has set His seal on Him" (John 6: 27).

There is also the intangible, feel good portion of God that we bask in and serve onto our plates. Those intimate, quiet times alone with the Lord are like aromatic, bath salts that turn ordinary water into a luxurious experience. The silence and the patient waiting on our Lord have a sweet, delicate flavor of their own. The comfort and the peace that surpasses all understanding not only have an appetizing aroma, but they taste better with every bite that we take. We are sure to look forward to the sweet fruits of the Spirit at the end of the buffet line of life when we take in all that we can of our Lord. *"But the fruit of the Spirit is love, joy, peace, longsuffering, kindness, goodness, faithfulness, gentleness and self control. Against such there is no law"* (Galatians 5: 22, 23). There is no limit as to how much of His fruit we may enjoy.

God's unlimited pleasure consumes your heart when you follow His lead and draw near. There is nothing more intimate or powerful than a heart to heart encounter with your Maker.

CLOSE TO YOUR HEART
It is true... You burst forth in love and joy over me.
I see Your buttons of gold upon Your chest,
Bright, almost blinding... so bright.
I watch as the buttons pop and burst
To expose Your heart of joy over me.
Never have I seen such splendor,
Never such a heart, never to see another like Yours.
I see true love... complete and unselfish,
Unconditional, pure and spotless,
Accepting of me and ready to draw me in.
I shall come near, step inside and come close to Your heart,
Never wanting to leave.
Never having to leave!

"You will show me the path of life; In Your presence is fullness of joy, At Your right hand are pleasures forevermore." (Psalm 16: 11)

Throughout the Bible we read about the character of God and all that He has for us. God offers us faithfulness, obedience, compassion, mercy, love, and much more through Jesus Christ. Hunger and thirst for God and desire Him because He is faithful to give. *"Ho! Everyone who thirsts, Come to the waters; And you who have no money; Come, buy and eat. Yes, come buy wine and milk without money and without price. Listen carefully to Me, and eat what is good, And let your soul delight itself in abundance"* (Isaiah 55: 1, 2).

Jesus is your eternal prize, your most prized possession. You belong to Jesus, and you have everything you need to draw close to God. God wants you to desire **Him** first and foremost without any hesitation. You are **His** most prized possession. God could have anything He wants; He is the King with clout. All the heavens and earth bow down to God. The Lord who created the world and the universe also has the power to create anything He desires to bring pleasure to Himself. Interestingly enough, all God wants is you and me; we are His first choice. God's desire is that we will crave true, lasting fellowship with Him. The Lord wants us to desire Him and pursue His attributes. God **is** altogether lovely, altogether wonderful, and He is winsome! Desire our Lord with all that you have. Pursue God and everything that He is and all that He stands for.

May your heart be filled with passionate flames of love for your Savior. May the Holy Spirit continue to fan those flames of love so that you desire more of God. May His presence within you grow and spread like wild fires to set the world ablaze for God. *"Trust in the Lord and do good; Dwell in the land and feed on His faithfulness. Delight yourself also in the Lord, And He shall give you the desires of your heart."* (Psalm 37: 3, 4)

Christian life. One summer day, it occurred to me that all of those good deeds prompted by my faith were pleasing to God, but they were not enough to bring me to the core of His being where I desire to be. I read the autobiography of Madam Jean Guyon who learned to live in the presence of God. I discovered that she used a significant ingredient in her life to escort her to that ultimate place of intimacy with God on a regular basis. Jean Guyon pursued God, obeying Him in a way that most of us haven't thought of doing consistently. She conquered her fleshly desires and her will in the ordinary circumstances of life. Jean struggled with life and tells of how she failed miserably time and again. Yet each time Madam Guyon found herself drowning in her own struggles to conquer her flesh, she chose to take the higher ground and start over with God's help. Eventually, Jean found herself able to travel down the secret path to God's presence and let go of her desires so that she would accomplish the will of the Father. She calls it abandonment.

Did she have to use the word, abandonment? What a frightening word that was to me! I wasn't sure that I wanted to explore her journey, but knew I had to take the necessary step to learn what Madam Guyon already knew. The dictionary would give me a proper definition for abandonment, but I was certain that I wouldn't like what it said. I imagined all kinds of things and conjured up painful feelings in my heart to confirm my fears of such a word. Thankfully the Holy Spirit, in His loving way, gave me a picture and an explanation of abandonment that helped me greatly.

The Holy Spirit showed me that abandonment works much

in the same way that a mother abandons her baby as the best thing for the child. The mother knows she can't care for the child and that leaving the baby on the doorstep of someone much more capable is the best solution for the child's welfare. She places the baby on the doorstep and turns away, never to return. Even though she is tempted, the mother does not go back and reclaim the child. She lives the rest of her life with the knowledge that she cannot go back; she did the right thing.

In a similar way, you and I have our own "babies" that might seem to be important but are not always best to hold on to. You might be thinking of one right now. Perhaps it is a desire, even something godly and good. Is it a plan or a hope for something better? There are many noble sounding things that I have carried or thought would be a part of my life that have turned out differently. We hang on to unnecessary baggage or wants because it feels right to carry them. It doesn't matter what they are; they've been with us for so long that they become part of us. Oftentimes, what we cling to hinders progress in pursuing a close, intimate relationship with the Lord. We surrender selfish dreams and desires unto the Lord, but God is saying that He desires true abandonment.

I used to equate acts of surrender with abandonment and interchanged the words often until the Holy Spirit showed me that there is a difference. Surrender comes after I've been fighting, and I creep out of my hiding place on the battle field. Clenching my teeth, I hold up the surrender flag with reluctance and wave it to and fro. It usually happens when I am forced to give in, and then out of frustration, I surrender into unknown territory.

I usually do this with a bad attitude, subconsciously looking for ways to take it all back and slip into hiding once again, waiting to return to battle. Surrender doesn't usually bring peace or contentment, and I feel like I've lost the war. There is no feeling of happily ever after, only resentment as my "baby" was yanked away from me when I lost the battle. It's amazing how many acts of surrender I have engaged in and then took back. God, I give my selfish pride to You, and to prove it I'll hold up the surrender flag. Oh, but Dear God, I take it back just for today when I go out into the battle field and have to be right. I will surrender it back to You later on when I am finished with it.

Does that sound familiar to you? It happens more than I like to think about. I find myself with weary arms and sore muscles from waving the heavy flag of surrender over and over. The flag becomes tattered and soiled from over use. Surrender can be a pitiful state of mind. Until the Lord helped me understand abandonment, I was probably the one out there with the most wear on my teeth and the sorest muscles from all of my attempts at surrender.

Surrender was not taking me into the throne room of God on a regular basis, so I chose to allow the Holy Spirit to work in my life to begin to understand and desire genuine abandonment. A close friend listened to me complain and express my fears over abandonment. I dreaded writing about it because I knew I would have to come to terms with it. It seemed like a radical word and a drastic thing to do. I had failed miserably at numerous acts of surrender, and I knew something had to change. Abandonment had to be an essential ingredient in my life if I was ever going to flourish in the presence of God. Yet I still anticipated the worst and thought only of the pain and suffering that might go with abandonment. Would I feel deprived and lonely? Would I suffer as Jesus did?

Anxious thoughts and questions kept me from seeking God and His peace concerning abandonment. I wasn't able to go forward in my pursuit to live in the presence of God. My deepest desire was once near and attainable, but then all of a sudden the awareness of God's continual presence seemed as far away as it could possibly be. With sheer desperation I cried out to God, but I still had one contingency. I remember telling God that I was ready to explore abandonment but not ready to suffer or give up much of anything. Isn't it sad that I drew a bold line on the path, allowing myself to go only so far with God and not another step? How thankful I am for the patience of God! The Holy Spirit came to where I drew my stubborn line and helped me to cross over it and continue on my path in pursuit of God.

God's Spirit began to speak and remind me of the ingredients that must be in my life if I am to live in His presence. I went back to the beginning, praising God in an attitude of gratitude and pursued Him with intimate prayer and fellowship. God wanted me to remember how much I needed Him and to depend upon Him even more. I knew that if I really depended upon God then I would desire Him and His character in abundance. Then abandonment might not be as difficult as I anticipated it to be. God reminded me that it takes all of the ingredients to flow in His presence, not just one or two.

Beginning with the simple, plentiful ingredients, Christians eventually find themselves prepared to add in the rest of them.

Abandonment comes in good time when we are ready for it. God won't rip anything out of my life or yours. Nor will He cause turmoil and confusion. In 1 Corinthians 14:33, the Bible tells us that God is not the author of confusion, but of peace. Seek His presence, desire to live His way, and The Lord will bring about peaceful abandonment. I've never known of anyone to reach deeper levels with God and regret the journey. Instead, I recall thinking of how wonderful it must have been to get there. The resolve to live in the presence of God eventually produces a pure heart and holy attitude. Isn't that why each of us is pursuing God so fervently? In holy pursuit of God, abandonment presents itself as a gift to Him, fresh and holy. That is how God designed it to be. Complete union and fellowship with the Holy Spirit is God's idea, not ours. In the Bible, Paul ends one of his letters to the Corinthian church with this wonderful blessing, *"The grace of the Lord Jesus Christ, and the love of God, and the communion of the Holy Spirit be with you all. Amen"* (2 Corinthians 13:14).

Choose the inward path, go deeper, and find yourself at the core of God's being.

THE INWARD PATH

Words of love You bring me today.
Words of encouragement, strength and peace…
They come my way.
For You love me deep within the core of Your being.
You open the access path to Your heart…
The path not traveled by many, for there is a cost.
Please, that my love for You would be limitless,
Open and subject to You, leading me
To come by way of the inward path.
Joy comes… love, peace, and encouragement too!
For if I seek the inward path to Your heart
I will find the secrets, promises, and truths of Your Word
Come to life.
If I seek You this way, I will have all that You desire for me.
Please, that You would open the access to the inward path today.
Please, Dear Lord, that I may travel and seek after Your heart
For it is open to me.

"Your word is a lamp to my feet and a light to my path."
(Psalm 119: 105)

The main obstacle that prevents genuine abandonment is selfishness. We don't want to give up what feels good, even if it isn't right for us. Selfishness is often at the root of sin. Human nature demands that we seek our own fulfillment, and we comply wholeheartedly. Oftentimes we are not even aware of selfishness, and denial settles in. It's difficult to embrace that thought, but it does happen. We begin demanding and commanding as toddlers. Children learn to say "no and mine" without a bit of training. How does that happen? It's that sin nature, and it rises up in a dark cloud of stubbornness hovering over every age. When I look at rebellious tendencies no matter what age or stage of life, I see selfishness. It is my way or the highway. Selfishness is subtle and lurks in the heart undetected, unannounced. Many of us live with selfish attitudes and don't know it. It has a magnetic pull on life, and we are attracted to it. Only the Holy Spirit can reveal selfishness and break its power.

Add selfishness to the pride that wells up within each of us, and we have another reason why abandonment isn't prevalent in our society. We stomp our feet, demand our ways, point the finger, and reveal selfish pride. Selfish pride will root itself deep within the heart to suffocate and squelch anything righteous that attempts to sprout up along side it. Pride has to go because it hinders the work of the Holy Spirit within us. It inflicts hurt onto the ones we love most and renders a guilty verdict from a condemning, self-righteous heart. That sounds severe, doesn't it? It is severe, and it is sin in fine form.

I praise God for Jesus Who overcame all sin at the cross through His death and resurrection! Through the Holy Spirit,

God gives grace and power to those who humble themselves before Him in order to overcome even the most stubborn of sins. The residence of the Holy Spirit within each born again Christian is the assurance that sin and selfish pride can be abolished. God's Spirit brings the desire and ability to conquer sin and run from its repercussions. That is good news for us. The dark clouds of sin vanish, and God clears the air so that we can love and draw close to Him. In the Bible, one of the Pharisees asked Jesus a good question. *"Teacher, which is the great commandment in the law?"* Jesus had the perfect response. *"You shall love the Lord your God with all your heart, with all your soul, and with all your mind. This is the first and greatest commandment. And the second is like it: You shall love your neighbor as yourself"* (Matthew 22: 36-38).

Love God above all and then love our neighbor as we do ourselves; is that possible for anyone? Does love mean that we have to do things for God and others or just have warm, fuzzy feelings of love for them? These two commandments could be a lot of work! This could be time consuming or even all consuming. These days we barely have time to take care of ourselves and our families. What is God asking of us? Doesn't He know that there are only so many hours in a day? This is not something that we can simply hire out for. It's going to take a real effort, and that might not be good enough either. Love says put God and others first, and that isn't easy to do. We weigh the pros and cons and come up with something reasonable that will work and fulfill our duty to the first and second most important commandments. We automatically think of ourselves and draw boundaries even before we get a true grip on what Jesus is requesting.

What **is** Jesus asking? Does He want us to do something or just feel a certain way, or is it some of both? Maybe it's all about our actions with a scoop of feeling on the side. We think we have it figured out until we read in the Bible about the night of the Last Supper. Jesus said to His disciples, *"A new commandment I give to you, that you love one another; as I have loved you, that you also love one another. By this all will know that you are my disciples, if you have love for one another"* (John: 13:34, 35). Again Jesus commands that we love. What does the Bible mean this time? Is this where abandonment comes in?

Jesus loved perfectly without a hint of selfish pride or arrogance. He was God's only Son. As a king from royal stock, doesn't it seem like perfect love should have been automatic for Jesus? But Jesus came as a man, a human like you and me. In Hebrews chapter two, the Bible says that Jesus had to be made like His brethren, that He might be a merciful and faithful High Priest. He didn't take His rightful place on this earth as an earthly king would do. Jesus shared in the suffering of others; He was right there in the thick of things with the worst of sinners and those most needy. Jesus was busier than any of us with day to day, moment to moment demands on His life. He had a job to do and prophecy to fulfill. God had a plan for His life just as He does for us. Jesus grew tired and weary, and He was tempted in every way just as we are, but He chose not to sin. *"For we do not have a High Priest who cannot sympathize with our weaknesses, but was in all points tempted as we are, yet without sin"* (Hebrews 4: 15). Jesus felt everything we feel, but He abandoned His rights of kingship and dealt with life just like you and I have to do. Jesus loved perfectly and left a flawless example of love to imitate. When I think of the commandment to love and then look at the life of Jesus, I see perfect abandonment. Throughout the gospels Jesus demonstrated abandonment.

It is impossible to love as Jesus loved without giving of ourselves and letting go of selfishness and pride. Jesus could have played the role of the righteous king, snapping His fingers at the disciples, requiring obedience to every command and whim. He could have looked out for Number One! Instead, Jesus was subject to the Father God. It's as if the robe that Jesus wore had oversized pockets at both sides. I picture Jesus pulling His pockets inside out, hanging them on each side of His robe to empty out all of their contents as a sign to the Father that He had no ownership in life, nothing belonged to Him. It was not the will of Jesus as a king, but the will of God for Jesus as a man that was accomplished.

Sometimes I wear clothes with no pockets and sometimes with one pocket on each side. Then there are times when it feels like I am wearing cargo jeans or "painter's pants" because I have pockets everywhere with even a few hidden ones tucked inside the larger pockets. I carry all my heavy rights with me, bulging in the oversized pockets. Those rights and selfish belongings in my pockets weigh me down, and I can barely walk the path of righteousness set before me. Even though I am burdened with the heavy load, I am too prideful or selfish to stop and empty the bulging pockets. Their contents represent my rights to security or stability, and even earthly comfort that I am reluctant to leave behind. Security, stability, and comfort are nice to carry around but only when Jesus puts them there. When I pull out my pockets and empty out the heaviness of the world to abandon my rights, then I find myself breezing down the path of righteousness that God has set out for me. The entrance to the throne room of God is in sight and much more accessible when I set myself aside in abandonment and love as Jesus taught me to love. I know it is God's will for me and for every Christian.

What should be done with the contents of your pockets once they've been emptied out? That is the perfect time to place them at the foot of the cross of Jesus Christ where they belong. Then turn your back and walk away, never to retrieve them. That is true abandonment. Like the young mother who can't care for her baby, give your selfish pride and your will over to Jesus, knowing that you can't drag it along and still live in the presence of God. Leave your heavy rights at the foot of the cross, and don't look back. This probably sounds like a good idea but an overwhelming task at the same time. That is why abandonment is the last ingredient necessary to learn to live in the presence of God. Be reassured; you will be able to do this.

Experience the love of God, and it will thwart every kind of evil to further your journey within the depths of Christ's love.

COMING FROM LOVE

Your love for me and mine for You
Will drive away a multitude of evil.
For where there is love, there can be no evil.
I shall love with all that is within me...
Heart, soul, and mind.
You cause my very being to rise above
The superficial love of this world that I live in.
You cause me to go deeper
To the same realm of love that Your Son operated in...
Selfless, abundant, and graceful.
What wonder comes from such love, a cherished possession,
A gentleness as I have never known, a peace not ever imagined,
And a joy to keep me going in times of trial.
No trial shall detain me now!
Most of all Your love draws me closer to You.

"... that you, being rooted and grounded in love, may be able to comprehend with all the saints what is the width and length and depth and height...to know the love of Christ which passes knowledge; that you may be filled with all the fullness of God." (Ephesians 3: 17-19)

By the time you are ready for abandonment, you've practiced living in an attitude of praise and gratitude while diligently working on a great communication system with the Holy Spirit through prayer. God is at the top of your desire chart, and dependence upon Him has become a way of life for you. You are ready to give God what He desires, total abandonment. The key here is that you must come freely and not expect that God will force anything from you. It is like letting go and allowing God. There is no tattered flag of surrender or jaw pain from clenching your teeth. Fists full of rage that once held pride and selfishness automatically relax and unfold. They fall to the side and naturally slip into your pockets unloading everything that weighs you down and keeps you from God. You face the cross of Jesus Christ in selflessness and realize that you are closer to Him than ever before. Great peace comes when you allow yourself to practice abandonment.

"Peace I leave with you, My peace I give to you; not as the world gives do I give to you. Let not your heart be troubled, neither let it be afraid" (John 14: 27). These are the words of Jesus to His disciples. They were spoken as words of comfort because Jesus knew that He would be leaving this world to send the Holy Spirit to be with His followers. It was a mysterious time of uncertainties for the disciples as they struggled to comprehend what Jesus was saying. It was not until later that they had some understanding. Practicing abandonment leaves us with uncertainties. We don't know the exact outcome. When we let go, what will happen? Is everything suddenly going to be alright? Do we naturally flow with God in complete joy? Will we instantly step into God's

everlasting presence here on earth?

While we can expect great peace in abandonment, we will experience some pain as well. Let's go back to the young mother leaving her baby. It is not something that she does without a degree of pain or sorrow. It's never easy to abandon anything we love, especially sin because subconsciously sin feels good to us. Even though we know it is the best thing to do, we will grieve a bit. In letting go there is a price to pay and some suffering that goes along with it. You might be thinking that this is where you'll get off the path and go back to where it feels more comfortable. Remember, by now you are ready for this last ingredient to help you live in God's presence. We are not to let our hearts be troubled or afraid. Jesus said, *"Let not your heart be troubled; you believe in God, believe also in me"* (John 14:1). The Holy Spirit is with us and will comfort and assure us that we have done the right thing in letting go of ourselves in abandonment, and there can be peace in the midst of the pain.

How intense will the pain be? Is there a quick remedy for it, something we can take every four to six hours around the clock to ease the pain or perhaps eliminate it? I don't know of such a remedy, and even if there is one, it is not the way to go. Jesus said, *"If anyone desires to come after Me, let him deny himself, and take up his cross, and follow Me"* (Matthew 16: 24). Did Jesus have to say it that way? Surely there must be an easier way. You might know other Christians who haven't done it quite like that, yet seem to have a good relationship with God. But if you have come this far, then you are probably not satisfied with merely an average or good relationship with God. You desire something deeper and more intimate, a perpetual encounter with the Living God that goes far beyond good. It is God's desire, and He is ready to dig deeper with you. You are prepared to travel to deeper levels of intimacy. That is why the next step, which involves discomfort, is really much more of a privilege than something to fear and turn away from.

A life of genuine fulfillment with the Author of Love awaits anyone who is willing to go the distance. Isn't that enough to pour out your willingness, let go, and trust that God will neither leave nor forsake you on the journey? It is enough for me, and it is my hope that it is enough for you as well. There is the temptation to escape and settle for less than God's best, but do not succumb. Take true comfort in this Bible verse that reveals more of the reality of Jesus because He feels burdens just as we feel them. *"For in that He Himself has suffered, being tempted, He is able to aid those who are tempted"* (Hebrews 2:18).

The Holy Spirit is there for you; He is the great Comforter and your most loyal companion walking with you every step of the way. When you live as Jesus, making every effort to find that place of intimacy with the Father, you will sense the Holy Spirit cheering you on. That doesn't diminish what you are dealing with. But the holy cheers from God do build strength and leave you with the feeling that you are not in this alone. *"I can do all things through Christ who strengthens me"* (Philippians 4:13). How many times have you read and quoted this beloved verse from the Bible? Do you really believe that every verse of the Bible is truth? If your answer is yes, then you are able to abandon whatever it is that gets in the way and keeps you from true intimacy with God.

Since it is Christ who strengthens you, He must be somewhere close by all of the time, totally accessible. *"Where can I go from Your Spirit? Or where can I flee from Your presence? If I ascend into heaven, You are there. If I make my bed in hell, behold, You are there. If I take the wings of the morning and dwell in the uttermost parts of the sea, even there Your hand shall lead me, and Your right hand shall hold me"* (Psalm 139: 7-10).

That is how it was with the saints of old who wrote in their journals about suffering and pain as they searched for the core of God's being. They relied on God to strengthen and sustain them as they trusted in His Word. Their focus was on God, and He never left them. Those who knew God had weakness and sin, but they also had strengths and special gifts just as we do. But in letting go, weakness and sin decreased while strengths and spiritual gifts increased. While letting go and allowing God, they found the secret to authentic abandonment. Their stories are left behind to encourage us.

Don't sulk in your trials or hide from them. Instead, abide in the love of Christ, and invite God to walk with you. You are much more than a conqueror, you belong to God!

FALLEN TRIALS
I am Your child
And still the troubles and sorrows of this world come my way.
You don't send them but You allow them to come
To mold and shape me to be more like You.
Oh, the imperfections of this fallen world!
You use them to shape my character too.
Your perfect love...it casts out all fear,
Casts out sorrow and unbelief, even trials.
Walking in Your love, I shall conquer trials.
A deeper love it is, yes bottomless!
So deep is my love relationship with You that
I shall cast aside an abundance of the world's imperfections.
Suddenly, beneath my feet
I feel the path of righteousness and obedience.
I am there and You are there on that path with me.

"Who shall separate us from the love of Christ? Shall tribulation, or distress, or persecution, or famine, or nakedness, or peril or sword? Yet in all these things we are more than conquerors through Him who loved us."
(Romans 8: 35, 37)

Abandonment is a personal matter between God and each one seeking His presence. Only the Lord knows what keeps each of us from His presence on a regular basis. Oftentimes we are merrily on the path unaware of obstacles, and God has to reveal them. For those of us willing to listen, the Holy Spirit is faithful to point out the road blocks that hinder our view of God. It is helpful to know what abandonment is not, so that you are not carried away into the deep end. Always remember that force is not involved. The Holy Spirit enables you to overcome hurdles but will never take control of your will and force abandonment. You will not have to play tug of war with God. Nothing gets yanked away without your permission; it is your choice to let go.

Here is what happened at first which made me fearful of abandonment. I was afraid that God might take everything away from me that I loved. Suffering is a painful word, and I dreaded it. I had questions and uncertainties. Would God play with my emotions and inflict something terrible upon me, leaving me to suffer all the days of my life of seeking Him? Would I burst out in spiritual tears with my soul downcast? Would it be unbearable, and would the price be too high to pay? I could have saved myself much grief if only I had placed my trust in the Lord and in the timeless words of the Bible. God loves me and would never do terrible or harmful things to me.

Instead, God met me just as I was, on the avenue of confusion that I had stumbled onto. The Holy Spirit told me that if I would let go of this or that, the quality of my spiritual life would improve. It was my choice to believe that this process was in my best interest, that God had something extraordinary for me or anyone who dares to take the step. I needed to focus on the Lord and not on myself. Somehow I started to see beyond myself and began to anticipate what God would do in my life. There were still road blocks of doubt and fear. In confusion and with uncertainty, I took a few detours, and the Lord had to re-route my steps.

Now after much trial and error, the more I trust, the more I see the faithfulness of God. When I watch for obstacles I usually discover them and have to make the choice to allow the Holy Spirit to strengthen me and remove them. As long as I'm human, there will be hurdles to overcome, but they don't have to keep me from God. I see the faithfulness of God as He meets me at each road block, and my faith travels deeper into His presence. I long for that forever experience of peace in His presence, indescribable. Would I trade the peace that surpasses all understanding for a quick, pain remedy to ease or eliminate my discomfort every four to six hours? Absolutely not! It is when I am weak that the Lord strengthens me and gives me peace.

There was a specific time when abandonment called, and the Holy Spirit had to do a work in my heart so that I would let go. My husband was spending quite a bit of time driving to and from work. He and I were the only ones living in our home where we raised Amber and Ryan; they are now grown. Mike asked me to consider "down-sizing" and moving closer to where he works. Leave the house we built where we established precious memories? Move from our great surroundings, friends, and conveniences? I wasn't about to move to an unfamiliar neighborhood far from my comfort zone. Needless to say, my response was not favorable, and Mike never mentioned it again.

But over the next six months, the Holy Spirit gently worked in my life to prepare me to let go of my house. I really didn't recognize that He was busy at work, but my selfish attitude changed. One day, Mike asked what I would like to do for the weekend. I replied, "Let's go and look at houses." He was shocked! It is a long story, but over the months, the Holy Spirit led to me a place of abandonment concerning my house. I was ready to let go of it…it was time to go. During the selling and moving process there was pain but also peace, just as Jesus promises in the Bible. Now our new house is home and feels like a gift from the Lord. I learned that I need to be more honoring of my husband's feelings and requests, but I also sense that God has a specific purpose for both of us in this new location and season of life. There is a broader perspective that I hope to discover. There was no pulling and tugging; it wasn't gut wrenching. It was a quiet, peaceful encounter with God when I let go, **and** I grew spiritually.

Leave your baggage behind, grab a hold of Jesus, and take the quickest flight from whatever hinders or blocks your spiritual pathway for living in God's presence.

A FLESHLY FLIGHT FOR LIFE

To die is great gain
For You accomplished Your mission that way.
Yet, You don't call me to suffer death on a cross.
You call me to open my heart to what matters most.
There are obstacles, they keep me from what matters most.
I must die to what hinders me.
Love will bring about death to my fleshly road blocks.
Love will overwhelm my own heart,
And the obstacles of the flesh shall fall away.
When I draw near to You, Your love takes me captive,
And the obstacles flee when I cling to You.
Not a wrenching process but a loving one.
When I abide in You, those fleshly obstacles that hinder me...
They flee.
This is true freedom, worth some pain
That I may come unto You.

"God resists the proud, But gives grace to the humble. Therefore submit to God. Resist the devil and he will flee from you. Draw near to God and He will draw near to you." (James 4: 6, 7)

When we think of abandonment we wonder what we will lose, but the opposite is true. We have everything to gain in genuine abandonment. We become more like Jesus, our flawless role model. In Hebrews 2:10, the Bible says that Jesus was made perfect in His suffering. During abandonment each spirit is more open to hear from God. When the fleshly obstacles are cleared out of the way, we have easier access to God and a greater ability to hear more clearly from the Holy Spirit. Just think of what life could be like if you could hear God's voice more clearly, moment by moment! When we know it is Him, there is incredible peace, and we are much more likely to trust and obey. It is simply a better way to live. Living in peace with God is a goal for every growing Christian. His peace leads to a place of personal contentment as well. When we let go and give God free reign in life, burdens are lifted, and the relief is incomprehensible.

Many Christians struggle with long suffering and adversity, searching for God's answers in the midst of tribulation. They wonder "**why**" they were dealt such a devastating hand in life. Faithful to pray, they send desperate petitions to God. They immerse themselves in the scriptures, meditating upon the Word of God. Hurting Christians seek wise counsel knowing God works through others. Those that encounter intense adversity also strive to overcome according to Biblical principles, sometimes to no avail. Eventually they stand firm, believing for the miraculous while exercising every ounce of faith they possibly can. Others who care, offer support and helpful suggestions.

Well-meaning advice comes from all around. "If you'd only do this or pray like that, don't let go of it…maybe you just don't have enough faith to get out of this pit" they exclaim! After countless efforts in search for answers and a happy ending, time goes on and nothing changes. The hopeless challenge is still on the front burner of life. Eventually battered Christians might question God's love and sovereignty. Guilt knocks, and they open the door to invite the idea that they've done something wrong. Despair and frustration settle in, and before long there is no hope for inner peace, no way out. What can be done?

We may never pretend to have the answers or understand why some faithful Christians experience intense suffering. This is something that only God knows for sure. In the Bible, Job was a righteous man. Yet he endured long suffering through a series of trials that many of us are uncomfortable even reading about. Most of us know Job's story of emotional and physical struggle, and we're afraid to relate to it. But it is helpful to stop and review his account in the Book of Job from the Bible. You might learn that Job's encounter with devastation is a powerful testimony of genuine abandonment. Job realized that it is better to live in the presence of God than to have answers. In the midst of what seemed to be never-ending turmoil, Job arrived at a place of abandonment. He came to terms with God and life. Job repented of any known wrong doing, he let go, and waited on God. Then Job enjoyed tremendous victory in God's presence. *"Now the Lord blessed the latter days of Job more than his beginning"* (Job 42:12).

How about you? Does it seem as if you have a never-ending cross to bear? Perhaps you have chronic illness or financial difficulties. Many suffer extreme loneliness and rejection. There are seasons of trials beyond measure. No matter what you might be dealing with, you can look at Job's testimony. You might not always know why you are dealing with your circumstances, but you can trust God. God desires for you to abandon whatever it is that is weighing you down; leave it at the cross of Jesus Christ and allow Him to take it from there.

God will draw you unto Himself in abandonment. You don't have to do it on your own. You will love as God loves, see as He does, and live in peace. Don't be afraid to let the Holy Spirit draw you. If you make a mistake, you are in good company. Go on knowing that those who learned to live in His presence failed time and again. By God's grace they made it and lived to tell their story. If you present yourself in complete submission to the Lord, what will happen? Perhaps in that humble state God will reveal the secrets of life eternal, and you will learn to have true and lasting communion with the Almighty. Embrace the entire ministry of our Lord Jesus and share in all that He did, even His joy in suffering. Leave your flesh at the crossroad, and allow your spirit to take the inward path that leads to the core of God's very Being. The lanes open up, traffic flows more easily, and you will arrive at your destination safe and secure, in good timing.

"And those who are Christ's have crucified the flesh with its passions and desires. If we live in the Spirit, let us also walk in the Spirit." (Galatians 5:24, 25)

A Blend of Ingredients

LIFE IN HIS PRESENCE...The Goal

It is the one who seeks You in everything,
The one who craves Your presence,
The one who searches for You in the busiest of day,
Yes, that one will find You!
That one knows the joy of Your continual presence,
The fullness of life.
The storms and the winds of life will not consume that one.
For You protect that one from adversaries.
Such protection, a fortress for the one
Who chooses to live with You.

As it was in the garden that splendid day when God first created man, it can be today. *"So God created man in His own image; in the image of God He created him; male and female He created them"* (Genesis 1: 27). God told man to multiply and be fruitful, and He gave him dominion over all that is on the earth. God had just created the entire world, but He saved His best for last. God gave man priority concerning the earth. He must have been extremely pleased and proud of His unique, perfect creature to extend such a privilege. Then God outdid all of creation when He gave man the ability to think, feel, and communicate of his own, free will. Man could do what nothing else in God's creation could do. God did a marvelous job! Was there a reason why God created man as He did?

We all know the story of Adam and Eve from the Bible. Oftentimes we remember their sin and separation from God, and the consequence that they paid is firmly deposited into the memory bank of every Christian. Now we live in a fallen world with many hardships because of the sin of Adam and Eve. But while we tend to focus on what they did wrong, we usually don't recall the unique privilege given to Adam and Eve, an ability to communicate directly with God in the garden. Yes, they had fellowship with God; they had it all. Everything that Christians strive for today, Adam and Eve had at their fingertips prior to their sin of disobedience. The ability to live in the presence of God was presented to them on a silver platter. God's heart burst with joy and excitement at the anticipation of fellowship with His new creation forever. Sadly, Adam and Eve disobeyed God, and their sin brought an end to garden intimacy with Him. We all know the rest of the story as we read on in the book of Genesis.

Each of us is affected by the sin of Adam and Eve. Because of them we were born without an automatic garden intimacy with God. In fact, the Bible tells us that we are separated from God and eternal life with Him unless we accept His only Son and be reborn spiritually. That is the gift of salvation through Jesus Christ that is freely available to every person who is born into this world. We don't have to do anything but believe and receive. When we receive the gift of salvation we are also entitled to the incredible gift that Jesus sent each of us, the Holy Spirit. The Holy Spirit takes up residency in our hearts, gently transforming each one into the person that God desires. It's as simple and as profound, as that. God's Spirit is always present. God **does** have a reason for the way He created you and me. God wants fellowship with us! We know from the Bible that we were created for such a purpose. The heart of God was content on the day that He created you and me.

Yet this sinful world is a challenge, and it's difficult to live in the continual presence of God. Obstacles block the pathway, and tribulation seems to barge in uninvited. The journey might become tiresome at times, but keep that constant desire and resolve to pursue God. For those who dig deeper and focus on God, there are rewards. God has heavenly secrets to share with anyone who desires to pursue Him with intimate passion. Sharing in the knowledge of God for the good of His kingdom benefits anyone who dares to seek Him. God is patiently waiting for you and for me.

What does it mean to live in the presence of God, and how

does it look in our busy world? We must keep in mind that Christianity is a relationship and not a religion. It isn't about laws or good deeds; Christianity is a lifestyle of fellowship with God.

Many Christians spend time doing things for God without getting to know Him intimately. Of course we don't want to diminish the need for Bible study and service in God's kingdom. It is the responsibility of every Christian to support the local church and mission programs that send the gospel forth throughout the world. The needy must be attended to. However, these acts of service must be a natural outflow of your relationship with God. Serving God has greater meaning and is much more fulfilling and effective when you are living with Him on a moment by moment basis.

When I think about God consistently, I am much more aware of His presence. It's something that I have to practice because the distractions of life shift my attention from one thing to another repeatedly. We all spend a fair amount of time in the car. For some, life is a never ending car pool and a series of errands, when oftentimes the front passenger seat is unoccupied. Why not take a spiritual ride and invite the Holy Spirit to occupy the empty seat next to you? You will need to practice single mindedness with the Lord's help, because you are more likely to focus on the cares of life or what is next on the list of errands. The Holy Spirit will enable you to take those bothersome thoughts and distractions captive so that you can pay attention to Him. God wants our attention. When we do practical things like making it our purpose to put Him in the seat next to us, He will start to seem more real. We will feel His presence more.

We spend more time than we realize focusing on personal problems and the troubles of the world. We gripe and complain and then whine about this and that. I've done it, and I still do unless I catch myself or make a choice to change my focus. We all face tribulation as part of this imperfect world, and I am not diminishing that. In John 16:33 we can look again at what Jesus said. *"These things I have spoken to you, that you may have peace. In the world you will have tribulation; but be of good cheer, I have overcome the world."* We've read that scripture many times and understand the truth of it, but how do we to appropriate it in real life?

That is when our relationship with Jesus Christ comes in. When the goodness of Christ is our focal point, we naturally think of numerous times when we've come through trials into His victory. One victory leads to another, and eventually we anticipate victory in His presence time and again. We don't wallow in sorrow but choose to look to the Higher Source and trust Him. When trials come to the surface, it's always a comfort to have someone available who is trustworthy and in whom you can confide. You can discuss past victories and pray together. Then the Holy Spirit supplies the faith to believe for more. This practice helps to bring you into the presence of God as you focus on Him.

When I think of God and all He has done for so many, I rejoice in the blessings and victories that are too numerous to recall. My pastor, JR, is filled with spiritual insights and wisdom, and he encourages our church to celebrate victories no matter how insignificant they might seem. He says that when we celebrate victories, we increase our faith and joy from the inside out. We will have more endurance for the next time because the Lord becomes our strength. Celebrating victories also releases God's power because God inhabits the praises of His people. That doesn't mean we have to have a cook-out and invite everyone over each time we celebrate. If we did that we would be entertaining all of the time because when we look for victory we will find it everywhere we go.

While it might be fun to throw a party to celebrate a big victory and share what God has done, we can also celebrate in simple ways on a daily basis. A prayer of praise and thanksgiving or a song unto the Lord is a celebration. *"Let my mouth be filled with Your praise. And with Your glory all the day. My mouth shall tell of Your righteousness and Your salvation all the day, for I do not know their limits"* (Psalm 71:8, 15). Acknowledgement of God's goodness to someone you know is celebration. The choice to focus on victory is a victory in itself.

When you focus on victory you can literally fill your day with praise unto the Lord. Did you know that getting out of bed in time to be ready for your day is a victory if you didn't get as much sleep as you needed the night before? You are exhausted from a long day but managed to get to the soccer field to love and support your child. That is a victory; celebrate it even for just a moment. Every time that you have dinner with the family there is victory, especially when life is so fragmented and hectic. Whenever you make family time a priority, you have tremendous victory. You are actually celebrating God, His provision and presence in your life when you acknowledge even the slightest victory. This will help you live in an attitude of gratitude that we have discussed numerous times. *"Finally brethren, whatever things are true, whatever things are pure, whatever things are lovely, whatever things are of good report, if there is any virtue and if there is anything praiseworthy...meditate on these things"* (Philippians 4:8). This is my very favorite scripture because I am inspired and strengthened to remember the good things and thank God. Are you beginning to realize that there is plenty of opportunity to remember God? Ponder God and talk to Him. It makes living in His presence seem more reasonable, doesn't it?

Give God your heart of gratitude and step into His presence. Enter in and marvel at His beauty and love for you.

DWELLING PLACE

How lovely is Your dwelling place!
Splendor and love penetrate Your very place of being.
I cannot comprehend the contentment
When I establish residency
In Your dwelling place.
But I anticipate and long for You there.
Your courts are open...
I will see Your heart and Your open arms.
Your desire is for all to enter in...
Room enough for everyone.
Oh, that the world would see Your heart
And know Your desires.
You are tangible, accessible; Your love is close.
You say,
"Come, enter into My dwelling place, My courts, My heart,
My love!"

"He who dwells in the secret place of the Most High shall abide under the shadow of the Almighty. I will say of the Lord, 'He is my refuge and my fortress; My God, in Him I will trust.'" (Psalm 91:1, 2)

Communicating with God is my favorite part about living in His presence. It is a staple of life for me and what I am most passionate about. As you know, when I learned that prayer is a two way communication system between God and me, I became passionate about my pursuit of God. Asking and listening is a way of life for me. Oftentimes I just listen, and I am amazed at how much the Holy Spirit has to say when I give Him the floor. When communication with God becomes more real, your relationship with Him will change dramatically and be much more intimate. In pursuit of God's friendship you will come to realize that life is more difficult without hearing His voice on a daily basis. Eventually you will work at hearing from God on a moment by moment basis. In 1 Thessalonians 5:17, Paul tells us to pray without ceasing.

Haven't we all wondered what that scripture is really saying? I remember times in Bible studies and home groups when we debated that scripture, and everyone had a different interpretation. We agreed that since the Bible tells us to pray without ceasing, then that is what we should do. How do I pray without ceasing, I wondered? Do I need to step into a spiritual state of mind or being? No one has time to "pray" all day and night. Certainly the monks and hermits long ago might have been able to pray without ceasing because they lived a life of seclusion, and they dedicated themselves to prayer and meditation. I had many unanswered questions. Years later, I have come to believe that this verse is simply instructing us to live in the presence of God moment by moment. When we are living with God, we are in fellowship with Him. Since prayer is fellowship with God, then we can pray without ceasing. God is with us all of the time.

It is helpful to stop thinking of God coming and going in your life. God doesn't visit and then leave only to return some other day or time. The presence of God is not a holy visitation but rather a moment by moment reality. Yet many people struggle to focus on the continual presence of God. Some have two lifestyles: a spiritual life on Sunday at church, and then another more secular lifestyle without a focus on God, for the rest of the week. Often I hear of how God came or how strong the presence of the Holy Spirit was at a certain time or event. Sometimes I even catch myself inviting the Holy Spirit to come and be a part of my quiet time. Actually, I think the Holy Spirit is asking you and me to come and be with **Him**! He is drawing each one into His presence. The Psalms are filled with melodious words that inspire us to live in God's presence more and more.

Often I hear the question, how do you hear God's voice? It begins when you accept Jesus Christ as your personal Savior and invite His Holy Spirit to live within your heart. You will not be able to hear God's voice or thrive in His presence if the Holy Spirit is not alive within you. Your mind doesn't register God's voice because your mind is not who you are. The definition of who you are lies in Jesus Christ within the depth of your spirit, your heart. The Holy Spirit dwells in your spirit, and this is the connecting place, where daily business takes place with God… Spirit to spirit.

There is not one, specific approach to recognize the voice of God. It does start with a genuine desire to hear and a willingness to practice listening. When I fill my mind and spirit with the things of God, I am more likely to hear what He has to say. In our culture, we are inundated with media where everything is available to us on television and DVD. Countless hours are spent listening to music that encourages no spiritual growth. Millions sit at computers for hours at a time surfing the internet, looking for bargains, and gaining knowledge about whatever is of interest. Children and adults of all ages are glued to the screen playing video and computer games. While these provide entertainment and enjoyment, they are serious distractions and can hinder spiritual development. Limit the time you spend on distractions no matter how well intended they are or how much enjoyment they bring.

Years ago there was a clever slogan that said something about how we are what we eat. This was a nutritional ploy to bring about an awareness of what and how much we eat and drink. Journalists published the medical research revealing the direct relationship between nutritional habits and health. Decades later, the evidence is clear that experts were correct in their claim. I take that claim further and say that spiritually we are what we take into our minds and hearts each day. What you read, listen to, and think about, will mold and shape your spiritual growth and maturity. It is a guarantee.

When Mike and I first dedicated our lives to the Lord, we knew we needed all the help we could get to represent Christ and get to know God. We wanted Amber and Ryan to grow up knowing God as well. We chose to spend as much time as possible reading and studying the Bible. We listened to contemporary Christian music exclusively. There were certain Christian teachers who captured our attention and gained our respect, so we spent hours listening to their teachings in the car and at home together. We purchased books and literature that helped to build upon our faith and taught us more about how to pursue a relationship with God. We attended church on a regular basis and met with other Christians often. We prayed with them and discussed our faith every time we met.

Mike and I decided that whatever we would do to promote growth and spiritual maturity for ourselves, we would also do with the children. We were so excited about God that we didn't want Amber and Ryan to wait until they were adults to pursue God intimately. We trained them at young ages to listen for God's voice, and they did very well. We were very careful about what we watched and listened to. If it wasn't appropriate for our kids then it wasn't good for us either. Wanting to hear God's voice and know Him better drove us to fill up on the right things. That doesn't mean we lived a life of seclusion or exclusivity. We didn't lock ourselves or the children in the house never to see or listen to anything that was not spiritually edifying. We have always embraced a normal lifestyle where we live, work, and play in the midst of the busyness of the world around us. But we chose to believe that we would become whatever we put into our minds and spirits. It was an effort, but eventually it became a lifestyle that made a significant difference in our pursuit of intimacy with God.

The discipline of fasting and praying is not mentioned much anymore, but the Bible talks about it. We are familiar with the Sermon on the Mount. It is a powerful account of the heart of God as Jesus spoke on behalf of the Father to instruct the disciples and the multitudes on Christian behavior and attitudes. Jesus said, *"Moreover, when you fast, do not be like the hypocrites, with a sad countenance. For they disfigure their faces that they may appear to men to be fasting. Assuredly I say to you, they have their reward. But you, when you fast, anoint your head and wash your face, so that you do not appear to men to be fasting, but to your Father who is in the secret place; and your Father who sees in secret will reward you openly"* (Matthew 6:16-18). Jesus didn't say **if** you fast, He said "**When** *you fast.*" It doesn't sound like much of an option to me.

Fasting is part of life, something to be taken as seriously as the rest of the teachings of Jesus on that mountain hillside. Fasting brings the flesh into submission to the spirit. It says no to the flesh and yes to the spirit. Not many are called to a complete forty day fast as Jesus did, but we are called to some kind of fasting and prayer time. What you fast or how long is between God and you. When I take away the distraction of food and replace it with prayer and attention on God, I can hear the voice of the Holy Spirit in the midst of a hectic day. For some, fasting might be total refrain from food for a period of time. Others might choose to eliminate a particular kind of food or some favorite thing that is a distraction in life. Those with medical issues should always consult with a physician before fasting food so that their health is not compromised. Everyone is called to fast in some way, and adding prayer draws us closer to God. The flesh feels deprived, but the spirit is edified. The voice of the Holy Spirit is much clearer, the rewards are plentiful, and the presence of God is sweet.

One of the most difficult things for busy people in a time-demanding society is the ability to sit still. You would have to agree that we are on the go most of the time. Even at home we're generally busy. Whether work related, homework, housework, television, or whatever… we tend to go until we crash in bed. How do you fill up on God and hear His voice when life is so full already? It takes an effort, but it can be done. Be willing to stop, be quiet, and give God your undivided attention. You might be thinking that this is where you want to get off the path and forget this whole pursuing God idea. After all, I did say that we could live in the presence of God even in our busy worlds. How can we be busy and be quiet at the same time?

If you are thinking that you can't afford to sit still and get to know the Holy Spirit then you will probably not learn to hear His voice consistently. Psalm 46 verse ten says, *"Be still, and know that I am God."* It could begin with five minutes of complete quiet and eventually build up to longer periods of time waiting on God. Meditating on a verse of Scripture is a good thing to do in that quiet time before the Lord. The Holy Spirit will guide anyone who desires to learn to listen for His voice. Don't be frustrated if you don't hear from God right away or even every time you stop to listen. It takes time and trust to cultivate an intimate relationship with God. The most important thing to remember is that you are giving God your time and that you are on His agenda…still…waiting on Him. It becomes a discipline, but unlimited rewards come from this quiet waiting.

God invites you to come near; He is drawing you. Run into that place of being where you encounter the Lord and His abundant love for you.

CORE OF YOUR BEING

You invite me to come near
To gaze into the inner core of Your being,
A look into what You are truly about.
I see love in purest form, untouched, unblemished,
As if refined
In the finest of fires.
Love in Your presence is the key, the secret and the answer.
Draw me inward with You at the core of Your very being,
To be transformed.
My fleshly ways will melt like wax.
Indeed my life becomes what You desire it to be.
Sin falls away, love takes over and...
Secrets of Your existence and joy flow as never before.
You await my visits to Your chamber,
Within the core of Your being.

"One thing I have desired of the Lord, That will I seek: That I may dwell in the house of the Lord All the days of my life, To behold the beauty of the Lord." (Psalm 27: 4)

Several years ago I felt like God was telling me to begin to desire a quiet life for our family. What a radical thought! Amber and Ryan were in grade school, music, and sports; life was hectic. Mike had a demanding job, and we were happily involved in the leadership of our church and its various ministries. We couldn't possibly develop a quiet life; everything we were doing was necessary. What was God asking of us? My first thought was scary. Perhaps we were being called to live in a small, remote town in the mountains and live off wild berries and Rainbow trout. I hesitated to tell my husband about God's desire for us, fearing that he would be overly excited since he enjoys fishing very much. Surely before the end of summer I would be sautéing fish and making wild berry jam!

I am embarrassed to say that I kept God's request to myself and didn't tell Mike. Finally one day I felt like I needed to tell him what I had been hearing from God. I blurted it out with great emotion when I told my husband that the Holy Spirit had directed me to desire a quiet life for our family. I promptly offered to pack our bags and move to the mountains. I was surprised to learn that Mike had heard the same words from God and was afraid to tell me as well. The word was out, and we were both relieved. What were we to do? Thankfully, my husband isn't as outwardly emotional or as dramatic as I can be, and he had the wisdom to ask God what He meant by "a quiet life." We prayed.

The Holy Spirit reminded us of how desperately we desired to know God and hear His voice but that we had allowed the busyness of life to get in the way. We were doing so many valuable things that we didn't have time to sit before Him and pursue the relationship that we longed for. It was time to clear out some of the clutter. God wasn't calling us to berries and fish. He was asking us to set ourselves apart from the distractions of life, yet live in the middle of the chaos in the world. It seemed like an impossible task. Thankfully, we've learned that when God says to do something, we must obey.

Over a period of time, with the guidance of the Holy Spirit, we figured out how to clear out some of the clutter. We said **no** to the things we didn't need to be involved in. At first it felt like we were about to desert everyone and shirk off our responsibilities at church. None of that happened. Eventually we felt comfortable with our new lifestyle, and our family was happier together. God had been preparing us for this new season in our lives. We made time for God again, and those years when our family lived a quieter life were some of our happiest ever.

During those quiet years I also dealt with inner struggles. My friends were very involved in their church programs. They were going to women's retreats, planning church luncheons, and were out doing the work of God's kingdom. Other friends and their families were involved in Bible studies and home fellowship groups. They were all being productive for the Kingdom of God. My mind and emotions were telling me that I needed to do all the things they were doing, but my husband and my heart were encouraging me to keep quiet. We didn't retreat from life, church, or fellowship, but we cut out some of the busy work and obligations we had. Our lack of involvement in the church programs was beginning to affect me in a negative way. I allowed guilt to pour into my mind and emotions. I believed that in order to be productive for God, I had to be "highly involved." It seemed like everyone around me was growing in the Lord because they were doing the things that I thought caused growth and maturity. Countless times I would go to Mike and suggest that we start this or that or do something significant for God. Each time he reassured me that it was not God's timing for us yet.

A few years went by before we felt like it was time to get involved again. We had an opportunity to work with high school students. Our quiet life was suddenly not so quiet anymore. It was good, though, because it was God's timing. We were rested up and ready because in those quiet years we learned to listen to God more. Sadly, I assumed that since we were involved in one thing that it was time to jump back into everything else again. I thought I was ready to resume all the other activities in addition to what we had just begun with the high school. That was not a safe assumption to make.

Thankfully, I am married to a man who is a sensible leader. Mike was not reluctant to help me draw a few boundaries for myself when he sensed my attempt to run full speed ahead. We were happy and content with what we had learned in those quiet years. We couldn't go back to the chaos of doing **everything** just because others were doing it or because there was a need. My husband reminded me that Biblical integrity with an attitude of excellence in every area of life is of great value to God. Too many commitments could compromise that. "Our current involvement is enough and in line with God's plan for us right now" he said. Again, I wrestled with my mind and emotions and struggled with all the same issues. It seemed like everyone else was being spiritual; they were doing all the spiritual things, and I was not. I desperately wanted to be a part of those kinds of activities. Out of respect for my husband and his wisdom, I let it all go, hoping I would learn something. What I learned steered me around a turning point in my life.

I learned to depend upon God. What a simple concept! While we never stopped attending church and fellowshipping with other Christians, we were quiet on the volunteering frontier. Volunteering and filling a need always made me feel like I was accomplishing great things, and it felt good. To pull back a little felt like I was underachieving and lacking in the area of Christian responsibility. I had to depend on the Lord for self-satisfaction. God had to be the One to make me feel like I was serving enough. That might sound like a simple thing, but it wasn't easy for me. All the while, I could see spiritual growth in others around me as they were telling me about what they had learned in various areas of service, and I wanted to share their same excitement.

The Holy Spirit had to become my excitement. I learned to yield to God, allowing Him to give me that worthwhile Christian feeling. Instead of getting up early to go and teach a Bible study or do some other act of service, God had me sitting in my chair meditating on Scripture, praising Him, and listening for His voice. At the time I felt like a free loader, sponging off of God without going out there to do my duty. I learned to trust the Holy Spirit, that God had a perfect plan for me. As we discussed earlier, trusting God and depending on Him doesn't always come naturally. Abandonment of my will was difficult and painful.

God was preparing me to learn to live in His presence.

I was finally starting to really understand why trust and dependency upon God are essential ingredients for a life that is spent with Him. While we have much to gain from Christian leaders and many others, there is no substitute for true dependency upon God. Jesus was totally dependent upon the Father for everything. Throughout the gospels we learn of how dependent Jesus was upon the Father. For us, it's like being little children, loving God and depending upon Him. In our busy lifestyles we make quick decisions and go on to the next one. We are conditioned to look for a good feeling and a quick fix on every avenue of life. We don't always take the time to practice asking God what **He** thinks.

The Bible has something to say about what God thinks. In Isaiah 55:8, 9 the Bible says, *"'For My thoughts are not your thoughts nor are your ways My ways,' says the Lord. 'For as the heavens are higher than the earth, so are My ways higher than your ways, and My thoughts than your thoughts.'"* Our Lord always has a valid opinion concerning each situation we face. God waits for each one to call to Him as a daddy and inquire of Him and His wisdom. God's ways and thoughts deliver happiness and contentment at the front door of the heart when we depend upon His input. It might seem impractical, but the Holy Spirit is ready to be a fresh part of each decision we make no matter how trivial. Every time we inquire of the Holy Spirit we draw closer to God more quickly than when we go off on our own. Dependence upon the will of God ensures more time with Him no matter what the question or the circumstance.

How can we possibly remember to ask God what **He** thinks? We have unlimited thoughts and tons of pressure to make decisions on a daily basis. It's difficult for anyone to remember to check with God throughout the day when not in the habit of doing so. But God meets us right where we are. Make it a point to inquire of God just once each day, and decide to trust and depend upon Him for the answer. Start there; you will make steady progress. It means practicing a little patience, unafraid to be vulnerable before God when you need direction. Practice yields spiritual freedom to depend upon God for everything. It's what Jesus did, and it is God's will for you.

There are those I've leaned upon over the years who have become near and dear to my heart. Throughout some of life's challenges they were pillars of strength and encouragement for me. Yet I drained them of time, energy, and wisdom in seasons of need. Their love and support has been invaluable, but with human limitations my faithful loved ones grew weary of my burdens. Likewise, I've done my best to be there for others with the same limitations. Surely you can relate to that. We desire to help, pray, and give advice, but it can be draining. That doesn't lessen the supportive roles we have with friends, family, and other Christians. Love and support are part of living in the body of Christ. It is scriptural to help one another and give words of wisdom and advice just as Jesus did. But we need to know our limitations, so we won't grow weary and become ineffective. We must also know when to stop giving advice and point those in need to Christ. The Holy Spirit will take it from there.

The Holy Spirit never grows weary. God's Spirit is a never ending source of strength, comfort, and direction for every Christian. It takes practice to learn to depend upon the Lord for everything, and it requires a great deal of willingness to yield to God instead of our own independent ways. The risks are minimal, but the benefits rise to the top of the charts. The practice of dependency upon God in day to day happenings brings the Holy Spirit up close and personal, involving Him in the complete circle of life.

Dependency is a matter of trust. Am I willing to trust that God just spoke and answered my question? Do I believe that if I seek and trust God, He will be faithful to come to the front lines of the battle ground on my behalf? Will there be someone to pray and help confirm what I think the Holy Spirit said to me? What if I put all of my trust in God's basket; will it amount to anything? The Bible says this: *"Trust in the Lord and do good; dwell in the land and feed on His faithfulness. Delight yourself also in the Lord and He shall give you the desires of your heart. Commit your way to the Lord, trust also in Him and He shall bring it to pass. He shall bring forth your righteousness as the light, and your justice as the noonday"* (Psalm 37:3-6).

God has given you the green light. Go with God, and grow with Him as well. The true, Christian character you desire can flow through every vein and vessel in your body. Jesus bulges out all over! There is an increasing desire for the presence of the Holy Spirit and an unquenchable thirst for all of God that you can have. Living in an attitude of gratitude with praise and worship overflowing from the heart, leads to an intimate communication system with our Lord. Continued fellowship with the Holy Spirit brings nurturing and trust into your relationship with Him. Trust in God ushers in dependency upon Him more each day. Before long you will crave the faithfulness of God as never before.

The Spirit of the Living God invites you to live with Him in the holy place of intimacy and be set apart for God. Listen… He calls you! Run…He's drawing you near!

HOLY HILL

To ascend the hill and stand in the holy place is Your presence.
To bask in the beauty of Your holiness…I achieve life's best.
Standing in Your presence, Your holiness is my goal,
The achievement of all achievements.
Nothing can be taken from me on that holy hill.
Upon that hill, I gaze upon the land and receive knowledge
From only You.
I see life as You do, through Your holy eyes.
This is what You have for me when I ascend.
I hear you call to me…
"Come, ascend and stand in My presence, never leave.
Set your feet upon holy ground, sink into the rich soil.
You will never be the same, never look back,
Or leave My presence."

"For thus says the High and Lofty One Who inhabits eternity, whose name is Holy: I dwell in the high and holy place, With him who has a contrite and humble spirit, To revive the spirit of the humble, And to revive the heart of the contrite ones." (Isaiah 57: 15)

Life is wonderfully full for those who desire God and His attributes. There is more on that plate than we can consume and digest in a lifetime. If we desire all of God that we possibly can and welcome the transfusion of His character, then we become irresistible to those around us. Somewhere, I once heard that we can't be contagious if we are not infected. Be **infected** with the character of God, and be fulfilled, more effective for His kingdom. Many who have not put their hope and trust in Jesus Christ watch with intensity to see how Christians behave and react to life. When the faithfulness of Jesus oozes out of your pores and you stand with His integrity ready to be His hands and feet, then to the watching world Christianity earns credibility. You'll find that some will come to you with questions concerning their doubts or unbelief when it comes to Christianity. It's true that others sense whom they can trust and turn to. You will be faithful just as Jesus is.

Every act of obedience unto the Father reassures others of your sincerity and your genuine nature. There is something attractive about obedience to God. Others can't quite put it into words, but they are naturally drawn to you. They sense honesty and sincerity about those who live in obedience to God. In Romans 6:16 the Bible says that obedience leads to righteousness. Obedience is a key issue with God. All through the Bible we read of those whose character and obedience were tested. The Bible says that those who were obedient to the Lord, were righteous before Him. I know we all desire to be credited as righteous before the Lord. Jesus is our righteousness. Taking on His character we become like Him, obedient unto the Father under all conditions.

It is interesting how one thing leads to another. Those who are obedient to God are molded and shaped to take on more of God's irresistible character. When we yield ourselves to God and respond with obedience, eventually we find ourselves acting and thinking differently, more like Jesus. Every act of obedience proves our trustworthiness, and trustworthiness earns us the right to become more effective for God. No one can be useful to God without the compassion of Jesus radiating from within. It would be of interest for us to sit back and take a look at how we might perceive others and respond to them when the Lord's compassion is flowing from each of us. It's amazing how much more tolerant and kind we are when we operate with the compassion of our Lord. The natural tendency to be judgmental or critical is tossed out the window.

Oftentimes, I pray and ask the Holy Spirit to show me how He sees certain situations or people so that I won't slip into critical, sinful tendencies. It is always a revealing experience for me. I've been able to see insecurity, lack of self esteem, fear, or other unfortunate qualities as the roots of adverse behavior. When I look at others with the eyes of Jesus instead of with my own judgmental and critical mind, I am moved with compassion. The more you stop and ask God for **His** perspective, the closer you will be to life in His presence. You will become more genuine and effective for His kingdom. When you move with compassion as Jesus did, you bear wonderful fruit.

Out of compassion emerges tender mercy. It is increasingly difficult to overlook someone or be insensitive and critical when we see them as Jesus sees them. That deep rooted compassion produces a merciful heart, responsive to the love of Christ. Instead of engaging in gossip and criticism, we find ourselves feeling the pain or inadequacies of those around us. A merciful heart changes the way anyone responds to others. We put to rest the arrogance that pressures us into old sinful habits of treating others poorly.

Oftentimes I hear idle excuses from others about how they aren't gifted with mercy, as if some are called to be merciful and some are not. Shortly after Jesus chose the twelve disciples, He began to teach them, and He spoke to the crowds. Jesus said, *"Therefore be merciful, just as your Father also is merciful"* (Luke 6:36). If you and I had been there that day we would not have taken the request of Jesus lightly. None of us would have gone home that day feeling like God created some to be merciful and some not. We are all called to extend mercy no matter how naturally bold or blunt we are. There are times when we're called to deliver a difficult message of truth. How much more effective do you think we might be for Christ if the delivery was coated with mercy? It's easier to accept a word of truth that is given with loving wisdom and a merciful attitude. Be the one who imitates the merciful nature of Jesus, and advance on the path of knowing Him better.

We know that mercy and forgiveness go hand in hand. You will find that it is much easier to forgive when you are operating with mercy. Without genuine forgiveness you cannot live in the continual presence of God. When you are stingy with forgiveness, you limit how much of God you are able to feast upon. Unwillingness to forgive opens a dark and dreary door where anger and bitterness come bursting through, ready to kill and destroy on contact. It is simple; God requires us to pardon others as we have been pardoned by Him. It is our Christian responsibility no matter what the circumstance or how we feel.

The Bible is loaded with scriptures about forgiveness, and it is clear what God thinks. Forgiveness is not a gray area in life; you must forgive as you have been pardoned. What a difficult task unless you've come down the path, and you already desire God so much that you would allow the Holy Spirit to infuse the characteristics of Jesus into your life! Then forgiveness becomes a letting go process, not a struggle. Forgiveness is abandonment, and it ought to be a natural response to the hurts and disappointments we encounter in this fallen world. The better you are at forgiving and letting others go, instead of holding them captive in your heart, the less pot holes you will fall into when traveling on the road that leads to God's continual presence. Before you know it, love is bursting out all over!

No one can love unconditionally in a true sense, unless they have weathered the storms of life and endured the journey. The greatest of all things is love; it is what remains when all else is gone. Unconditional love is one of the most powerful tools we have for building our lives to imitate Jesus. For those who choose to love as Jesus loved, there are great rewards. The greatest reward is the assurance that we have done what Jesus commanded us to do. Everything about the nature of Jesus is attractive, but of all His attributes, love is the one I desire most. I know that love will cover and overcome all.

The biggest surprise that I've encountered in this whole journey of life in God's presence is that loving like Jesus loves is not that difficult. I've always read the scriptures on love, and

I often meditated on the greatest commandment. Each time I came away with a new lease on love. I would be raring to go and love like Jesus only to fail time and time again. It wasn't until I began this journey of life in God's presence that I was able to learn to allow the Holy Spirit to teach me and love through me. This journey is a process, and I know that I still haven't arrived at my destination. I've had a taste of what it can be like, and it's mouthwatering enough to go back to the buffet for a huge helping of God's love and practice what I have learned.

Unconditional love and complete devotion to the Lord enable you to let go of yourself and yield fully to the will of God. It is comforting to know that God will not blindfold you and force you to walk the plank to a destructive fate when abandonment is your heart's desire. The Holy Spirit gently transforms you over time on your journey to life in His continual presence. It is never sudden or abrupt because the journey is too meaningful for that. What you learn along the way will carry you to the next stage. Everything about you is refined when you let go and allow the Holy Spirit to take control. I always have to remember that **God is God** and that I am not. God has all the rights, and I have none. The Lord has full authority to ask anything of me, and I have the responsibility to respond in submission and obedience.

Your contentment will never be contained when you journey on the road that is set before you, in the presence of God. The purpose for your life unfolds on that obedient path.

PATH OF LIFE

In Your presence... no greater joy,
No greater fulfillment, no higher high,
No better road than this path of life.
Life is abundance... abundance even more than I need.
I give from my abundance to those in need,
To walk the path of life.
The path of life is Your will set before each of us.
Walking the path of life, I share in Your joy.
My obedient heart gives You great joy.
I have great joy when my soul is fulfilled, and so
It shall be for all for eternity.

"Therefore my heart is glad, and my glory rejoices; My flesh also will rest in hope. You will show me the path of life; In Your presence is fullness of joy; At Your right hand are pleasures forevermore." (Psalm 16: 9, 11)

Having all of the knowledge is one thing; living it is another. That is why abandonment is one of the last ingredients to incorporate. When I am willing and committed to God, then He can mold and shape me any way that He chooses. Do I always have to be right or come first? Are my feelings most important? Is my pain greater? Do I need to have the attention or the last word? Does it have to be my way? These are some questions that I ask myself routinely. Sometimes I don't like my answers. There are times when I feel like I have failed the midterm test, and there is no hope for the final exam. Actually, there are times when I feel like I do a poor job on the simple quizzes along the way. But God is faithful, loving and kind, and He won't give out my final grade before it is time. Instead, God extends tender mercy and grace, and He sends His Spirit as my personal tutor as an assurance of my continued progress.

I've sensed God's patience and experienced His faithfulness in great measures while stumbling through the process of abandonment. Most importantly, I keep trying. When I fall, the Lord is always there to pick me up to begin again. I've noticed that longer periods of time go by before I fall again. Letting go and allowing God doesn't come easily for me, and I am guessing that it isn't that easy for you either. That sin nature tries its best to weasel its way into the center of intimacy with God and rob His children of righteousness. How thankful I am that Jesus has become our righteousness and that sin has no hold upon any of us who have spiritual rebirth into the Kingdom of God! That frees me up to pursue God and exchange my rights for His righteousness. Learning abandonment unto the Lord is a trial and error process, but you will make steady progress when you choose to let go and trust God. Instead of a loss of personal identity there is a gain of **lasting** identity in Christ. In letting go you have everything sinful to lose and all that is of God to gain.

Life in the continual presence of God is a fruitful life. Nothing should keep you from the beauty of an enriched life in Christ. The promises of the Bible pop up in three dimensional formations for you to grab and take hold of. God seems more real, and true Christianity becomes your life. You no longer hope that the Holy Spirit will show up because you have access to Him on a moment by moment basis. The Holy Spirit becomes your friend and closest confidante. Conversations with God flow like warm honey, and life is all about the Lord and getting to know Him better. Nothing is more important than your intimate relationship with God through the Holy Spirit because Jesus paved the path for you.

Does this sound unrealistic or too good to be true for you in a world consumed with busyness, distractions, and obligation? This **is** real life in its purest, most simplistic form, and it is what God desires. Some would say that it might work better when all of the kids are off to college or when retirement comes and there is more free time to pursue God. That is understandable and logical, but it isn't God's best for anyone. God will never tell you that it's too late, but He is saddened if you choose to let the pressures and urgencies of life keep you from the abundance that He has for you right now. We tend to think that pursuing God is only about serving and doing great things, so we'll get to Him when we have more time. We all place priorities in a specific order of value. For some, work is most important and family next, with a personal relationship with God after that. Others put their families first, their job next, and give their relationship to God third place on the list of priorities. No matter how you prioritize, your relationship with God comes first, **not** what you do to serve Him. The quality of your other priorities is always affected by your relationship with God. Focus on God first, and He will improve the quality of everything else in your life. *"But seek first the kingdom of God and His righteousness, and all these things shall be added to you"* (Matthew 6:33).

Don't you want to know the King and receive all that He has for you? Isn't it worthwhile to go the distance to find favor with God? Would you rather be on your own than be surrounded with an assurance of the power and presence of the Almighty every minute of each day? Don't you desire to do the very things that Jesus did? Don't be mistaken. This is not a candy coated, cookie cutter plan for success. It is the realization that you need Jesus Christ and the Holy Spirit's continual involvement in your life. It takes courage and humility to admit that you need a friend like the Holy Spirit. I have learned that I am nothing without the Holy Spirit's continual leading in my life. I can't take credit for anything, but I **can** give praise and glory to God for every good thing because it comes from Him. It is impossible for me to bless my own life; it must come from God.

There have been too many times when selfishness and independence have taken a front seat and shoved the will of God into the trunk. Painful labors over decisions could have been avoided if I had only pursued God and His presence in my life. Peace that surpasses all understanding would have warmed my heart if I had not worried, fretted, and distressed over issues. Even though Jesus didn't promise a life free from pain or difficulty, He did promise to send the Holy Spirit to be there each minute of every day to help and comfort us. God's Spirit makes all the difference.

Living in the presence of God with the Holy Spirit, lifts your spiritual life up into heavenly bliss. You can have a better garden intimacy than Adam and Eve ever had with God. You might face trials and experience what this fallen world has to offer. But you are not a victim, nor do you ever have to muddle through life alone. You have victory in Jesus Christ and the ability to live in the powerful presence of the Holy Spirit with constant access to God. You already have the assurance that it is God's will for you to live in His presence. Does anything else matter?

Each of us is well equipped to live with God. We have His Word from the Bible and other helpful materials to read and study from. We have the fellowship and support of Christians around us who lovingly hold us accountable. Godly virtues, principles, and standards are lofty pillars that have withstood the test of time, and they are still there to assist us. As always, there are numerous resources that you and I have in our individual lives to equip and continue to draw us closer to God. The ingredients that we have discussed in this book will serve you well when you take them seriously and practice them. Living with an attitude of gratitude in praise and thanksgiving unto God ushers in a spirit of intimacy for loving fellowship with God through prayer and communication. The celebration of your dependence upon God, trusting in Him, conjures up a craving for the attributes of

Jesus, and He becomes your heart's desire. Letting go in sincere abandonment unto the Lord sets you free, reaching the core of God's being. Most importantly, Jesus Christ is your personal Lord and Savior, and His Holy Spirit lives in your heart, providing perfect guidance. You have everything you need.

I have often wondered how it might feel to live in the continual presence of God. Will I be super spiritual or extremely holy? I have pictured my life to be one continuous conversation with God, oblivious to my surroundings. There have been times when I have imagined myself in a grocery or department store with my mouth going a million miles an hour talking to God. What if I become an extremist or a legalist and misrepresent Jesus Christ, driving others away? Will life be one continuous out of body experience day after day? Perhaps you relate to some of these questions. By now, we all have our preconceived ideas and dreams of what life might be like in God's continual presence. We desire to live with God, to access Him throughout the day and night in an intimate manner. What can His children expect?

Be assured, you won't feel like a spiritual giant, nor will you think more highly of yourself than anyone else. There's no room for arrogance because your identity is in Christ, and your humble heart is in true submission to God. You will engage in the world around you and do your part to help make it a better place instead of selling out to complacency. No one is going to single you out as if you are talking to an imaginary friend. Mercy and grace will be a natural outflow of the love of Christ, and others will be drawn to you. Reality stands at the forefront of your mind and heart, not out of your body, and your feet will be firmly planted on solid ground. Your life will be peaceful, meaningful, and fulfilling.

You will look surprisingly normal on the outside, but you will be transformed on the inside. Life becomes richer when you give praise and thanks to God and acknowledge the good all around you. You won't grow weary of prayer because fellowship with the Holy Spirit will provide refreshment continually. God becomes your ever present Source, and your complete faith and trust in Him will keep you coming back for more. The nature of Jesus Christ will be deeply embedded in your heart and mind, with more than enough of God to share with others. Letting go in genuine abandonment will bring lasting peace, and you will keep God on the throne where He belongs.

Living in the presence of God is life at its fullest. The desire to be with God is so powerful that pursuing Him becomes a life long passion. The one who chases after God will surely find Him and grow to immeasurable heights in Him. The Spirit of the Living God shouts from the mountain top of each precious heart with utter joy, in everlasting intimacy with His beloved, and…He is pleased!

"You will show me the path of life; In Your presence is the fullness of joy; At Your right hand are pleasures forevermore." (Psalm 16:11)

Enrich your spiritual life with this study companion to
Living in His Presence
Secrets in His Presence
Fresh Encounters with God

by Gina Moroney

An enjoyable journey in pursuit of intimacy with God

Learn to hear the voice of God
Discover peace in the midst of the storm
Watch as worry and fear melt away
Feel God's presence instead of loneliness

About the author

Gina has learned to trust and depend upon God. Through her failures and successes in life, she opened her heart to Jesus Christ and realized that Christianity is a relationship with God, not a religion. In her own personal experience pursuing this relationship, God revealed five essential ingredients that would help her live with Him, moment by moment. Now her daily conversations with God give her strength, comfort, support, and guidance in every aspect of life. Gina lives in Denver, Colorado with Mike, her husband of thirty years. They have two grown children. She treasures time with family and friends, skis in the mountains of Colorado, and enjoys cooking Italian delights.

www.ingramcontent.com/pod-product-compliance
Lightning Source LLC
Chambersburg PA
CBHW052034070526
44584CB00016B/2040